Meta
An Intro

Dad,
    This is one to exercise the old brain cells!
        Many happy returns,
            Paul.

Nov. 1987.

Modern Introductions to Philosophy

General Editor: D. J. O'CONNOR

PUBLISHED

OTHER TITLES IN PREPARATION

Metaphysics:
An Introduction

Brian Carr

MACMILLAN
EDUCATION

First published 1987

Published by
MACMILLAN EDUCATION LTD
Houndmills, Basingstoke, Hampshire RG21 2XS
and London
Companies and representatives
throughout the world

Typeset by Wessex Typesetters, Frome, Somerset
(Division of The Eastern Press Ltd)

Printed in Hong Kong

British Library Cataloguing in Publication Data
Carr, Brian
Metaphysics: an introduction.—(Modern
introductions to philosophy)
1. Metaphysics
I. Title
110   BD111

ISBN 0–333–32397–1
ISBN 0–333–32399–8 Pbk

CONTENTS

To Indira

PREFACE

'Metaphysics' was the title given by Andronicus of Rhodes, one of the earliest of the editors of Aristotle's works, for the writings which he placed after Aristotle's physics. The issues which now go under that heading are so wide ranging and richly if not exhaustively harvested by successive generations of philosophers that it would be an impossible task to really do the subject justice in a book of this length. I have tried, therefore, to do justice only to one approach to these questions which has its source in twentieth-century analytical philosophy, though advocates of this 'descriptive metaphysics' find it relatively easy to adapt large portions of the writings of many major philosophers of the past to serve their ends. (That indeed would seem to be the criterion for calling them 'major' philosophers – and clearly raises questions of intellectual and historical propriety, albeit answerable ones.)

I would like to acknowledge the benefit I have enjoyed of discussions at various times with students and colleagues at Exeter University, particularly Glenn Langford, of ideas and themes which have formed the basis of my thinking about metaphysics. I would like to thank Professor Dan O'Connor once more for his support and encouragement of this project and my wife Indira Mahalingam for discussing with me the issues of this work beyond the call of duty. I express my thanks also to Professor David Hamlyn of Birkbeck College, London, who kindly arranged for me a Visiting Research Fellowship there for the autumn and spring terms of 1985–86, which enabled me to bring this book to completion.

Brian Carr

CHAPTER 1   CATEGORIAL DESCRIPTION

I. INTRODUCTION TO METAPHYSICS AS CATEGORIAL DESCRIPTION

Metaphysics is one branch of Philosophy, but arguably more fundamental than other branches such as Epistemology (the Theory of Knowledge), Philosophy of Mind or Moral Philosophy. Sometimes it has received disparaging attacks as a noncognitive and hence nonsensical enterprise, a fate suffered notoriously during the present century at the hands of the philosophical movement known as 'logical empiricism'. Whether any such charge against it is just and fair depends however on quite what metaphysicians are up to, and it must be admitted that many such philosophers have had greater ambitions for their subject than seem in retrospect to be prudent. To reveal the true nature of reality, its contents and structure, to place man within the cosmos in his relation to other kinds of things and to his creator, to determine man's duty to himself and to God, and the true route to happiness – those are common enough ambitions, exhibited in the works of Plato, Descartes, Leibniz, Spinoza, Bradley and so on. No wonder its advocates have exalted the metaphysical pursuit!

There is nevertheless a relatively minimal metaphysical activity which can make claims to a legitimate and central place in philosophy, perhaps even to *the* central place, and which has always been part of the wider activity of metaphysicians. Even if it is questionable whether the existence of God, the nature of the spatiotemporal universe, and the future of the human soul can be investigated and established by rational argument, the metaphysical activity which I want to identify and introduce falls under no such grave suspicions. And though it is a minimal activity within the wider contentious one, it is not itself unrewarding.

Metaphysics, in its minimal form, is the activity of categorial description. Its subject matter is the most fundamental aspects of the way we think about and talk about reality, the most fundamental features of reality as it presents itself to us. We divide the world into horses and trains, people and mountains, battles and towns, and a whole complex structure of different kinds of things; our language is the repository of this enormously rich furnishing of the world. But we can discern within this richness some overall divisions, between things and their properties for example, or between events and the times and places in which they happen, and it is with the overall pattern of our categorising of elements of the world that metaphysics concerns itself. The basic divisions which our thought and talk about reality entail are the quarry of categorial describers.

To make this notion more precise, I will sketch out the results of such investigations by Aristotle and Kant. They have both important and instructive similarities and differences.

1. *Aristotelian categories*

In the short but characteristically difficult work now known as the *Categories*, Aristotle lists ten different categories or 'predicables' as follows:

> Of things said . . . each signifies either substance or quantity or qualification or a relative or where or when or being-in-a-position or having or doing or being-affected. To give a rough idea, examples of substance are man, horse; of quantity: four-foot, five-foot; of qualification: white, grammatical; of a relative: double, half, larger; of where: in the Lyceum, in the market-place; of when: yesterday, last-year; of being-in-a-position: is-lying, is-sitting; of having: has-shoes-on, has-armour-on; of doing: cutting, burning; of being-affected: being-cut, being-burned.[1]

Aristotle's categories are 'predicables' because (with reservations to be looked at later) they are things predicated of something: when we say, for example, that 'Socrates is a man' we are predicating being a man of Socrates, i.e. a certain kind of substance. Again, when we say that 'Aristotle is in the

Lyceum', we are predicating being in the Lyceum of Aristotle, i.e. a certain place, physical location. The ten predicables listed are the ten kinds of things that can be said of something. Now 'thing' is used here intentionally to convey the fact that Aristotle is, in the first place, talking about the world and not about language. It is being in the Lyceum as such that is predicated or said of Aristotle, not the expression 'in the Lyceum' which is (if at all, and certainly in a different sense of 'said of') said of 'Aristotle' the name.

But 'thing' is used also to convey another fact about Aristotle's ten predicables, namely that the list involves a division into ten types or kinds of what can be variously called 'things', 'entities', 'existents' or 'beings'. Socrates is one kind of thing, a substance, and so is Aristotle; in-the-Lyceum is another kind of entity, a place or location; four-foot is a quantity; white is a quality; yesterday is a time; and so on. Aristotle, in drawing up a list of the ten different kinds of things predicable of something else, is drawing up a list of the ten different kinds of beings, entitites, existents, or things. According to Aristotle we have to distinguish the categories of substance, place, time, quality, action and so on.

Now where does Aristotle get all this from, and is he right? As the remainder of this book involves an attempt to answer the latter question in outline, I will comment only on the former question here. How on earth could Aristotle have come up with this classification of things in existence in terms of ten categories? Clearly he did not engage in an empirical investigation of the things around him and arrive at his result as he would at a classification of species of animals or plants. The answer has to be that, insofar as the list is the product of investigation it was investigation of our *thought* and *talk* about the things which Aristotle could find around him. One commentator on Aristotle's list suggests that it was arrived at by distinguishing different questions which may be asked about something and noticing that

> . . . only a limited range of answers can be appropriately given to any particular question. An answer to 'where?' could not serve as an answer to 'when?'. Greek has, as we have not, single-word interrogatives meaning 'of what

quality?' and 'of what quantity?' . . . and these, too, would
normally collect answers from different ranges.[2]

Something along these lines has to be right, since Aristotle
could not have investigated reality directly, and that for at least
two reasons. One is that reality is not something which itself lies
beyond or prior to our thought and talk about it in a way that
allows of independent perusal, since reality is for us the very
thing which our thought and talk concerns. If that looks
tautological, let it be: a more substantial claim needs greater
argument than I can offer now. The second reason is that any
perusal of reality would need to rest upon a way of classifying
what is discovered in it: are we going to list places and times,
qualities and numbers, relations and events? Well, that
depends on the categories involved in our thought and talk. It is
the very result of category division in our thinking and talking
that the world divides up as it does. A way of putting this point
is in terms of perception. To perceive the world is not, as a naive
Lockean might think, to passively notice what is there; it is to
conceptualise and hence pigeonhole what is there. And
categories are the broadest, most fundamental and most
general of our pigeonholing devices.

2. Kantian categories

From this perspective it is quite understandable that Aristotle
should turn to the features of thought and talk to discern the
features of reality. How else could he proceed? Yet it must be
emphasised too that Aristotle's ten categories are listed as
categories of things in the world. Aristotle should be seen as
interested in the divisions which reality involves, even if he
must approach them indirectly through thought and language.
He did not subscribe to the view just expounded, but on the
contrary actually took his task to be the description of the
categories of being. In this respect, Aristotle and Kant firmly
part company.

For Kant, there are twelve categories to be listed, and he
divides them into four groups: the categories of quantity are
unity, plurality, totality; those of quality are reality, negation
and limitation; those of relation are substance and accident,
cause and effect, reciprocal interaction; and those of modality

are possibility, existence and necessity.[3] Now there are all sorts of differences between these categories and Aristotle's, and the lists of categories differ widely in form and content. There is a similarity, though, and Kant himself excused the use of Aristotle's term 'category' by saying that their primary purpose was the same – to list the fundamental concepts employed in our thought about the world.

Let us assume then that what is at stake are the divisions existing between different kinds of being, entity or thing. In the traditional designation of this study, let us assume that Aristotle and Kant are both attempting to sketch an 'ontology'. If so, we must allow that the terms 'being', 'entity' and so on are here employed in a very wide sense which allows for such peculiar 'entities' as possibilities, necessities, and pluralities as well as substances and causes. We need to adopt some general terminology for the enterprise of categorial description, and if we are cautious in our use of the terms there is much to be said for adopting this usage. Caution will be exercised in not assuming, indeed in positively denying, that substances and qualities are the *same* kind of thing, or that possibilities exist (if they do) in the same way as particular things.

How did Kant get his twelve categories, the twelve 'pure concepts of the understanding' as he called them? He certainly did not get them from a perusal of the world lying outside of and independent of our thought about it, for his official view of *such* reality was that it lay totally outside our ken. There is no way, he holds (for reasons going deep into his philosophical system), whereby we could attain any knowledge whatsoever about such thought-independent reality, and it follows that the list of categories has been derived from another source. That source is a natural one for Kant, since his categories are after all the fundamental features of our thought.

Kant's source is logic, the study of the different forms of propositions (or 'judgements' in Kant's more psychological terminology). He borrowed – albeit with some modifications – the list of forms of judgement from traditional logic, giving it as follows: the quantity of a judgement may be universal, particular or singular; the quality may be affirmative, negative, infinite; the relation expressed may be categorical, hypothetical, disjunctive; the modality may be problematic, assertoric or apodeictic.[4] Just how Kant gets from the list of twelve forms of judgement to his list of twelve categories need not concern us in detail. Suffice it to say that he discerns the application of the category in the use of its corresponding judgement form. For example, in making the judgement 'Socrates is wise' the predicate is related to the subject categorically, hence the category of substance is being applied: Socrates, in other words, is a substance. Again, in the judgement 'If you press that spot, I will feel pain' the hypothetical judgement form is being used, hence the category of cause and effect: pressing that spot is the cause of my feeling pain, the effect.

We can, by the way, already see one weakness in this derivation of the twelve categories. Not every judgement of subject-predicate form involves the category of substance, as for example is witnessed by the judgement 'Four is an even number'; and not every judgement of hypothetical form involves causes and effects, as is witnessed by the judgement 'If Tabby is older than six months, he is older than six days'. Clearly only the particular application, in the right way, of the twelve judgement forms to spatiotemporal phenomena is going to come close to ensuring the required relationship between judgement forms and categories.

But the important thing for us now is to stress that Kant is not going beyond thought to reality to find his categories. They are the fundamental forms of thought, embedded in the forms of judgement. This puts Kant in stark opposition to Aristotle for whom the categories, however identified, were natural, real divisions among things in the world. I will put this opposition by saying that Aristotle was a categorial realist whereas Kant was a categorial conceptualist. A categorial realist is someone who takes the categories, which he seeks to describe, as marking real kinds to be found in the things which collectively make up reality, and so takes categorial description as indistinguishable from (or at least an important part of) the grand traditional task of metaphysics. For the categorial conceptualist, the task is to describe the fundamental features of our conceptual scheme, of our thought and talk about reality, with no assumption made about the way reality exists independently of that manner of thinking and talking.

A philosopher might not follow Kant completely in insisting that the categories do *not* reflect features of reality as such, and yet still be a categorial conceptualist on this definition. And this is the position which is held by the philosopher who engages in what I am calling the minimal activity of categorial description: what are being described in this minimal metaphysical pursuit are the categorial features of thought and talk about the world, whether or not the world matches up to those features. Such a minimal pursuit is neither realist, as was Aristotle's, nor Kantian in its conceptualism in the sense of denying the adequacy of concepts to reality. Categorial description can go ahead without such assumptions.

3. *Collingwood's metaphysical relativism*
There is one feature which Aristotle's realist metaphysics and Kant's version of categorial conceptualism had in common which I want to indicate now, as not involved in the minimal pursuit of categorial description. This is best brought out by the example of a philosopher who adopts a position which positively rejects that feature.

Collingwood, in his *Essay on Metaphysics*, develops an account according to which metaphysics concerns the fundamental assumptions or presuppositions of the scientific thinking of an age.[5] The metaphysician's task is to lay bare these assumptions; such as, for example, the causal principle that events without exception have an explanation, made by deterministic science and not by non-deterministic science. Since science is never static, and since the fundamental presuppositions of science are subject to change as well, it is necessary to look upon the metaphysician's task as itself in principle an open one. Even were the presuppositions of science to be carefully revealed and documented, the task would need to be done again for another scientific age. There is no one final, unrevisable, true metaphysics for Collingwood: there is only the true description of the metaphysical presuppositions of the science of an age.

To give a position such as Collingwood's a name, I will call it 'relativism' as opposed to the 'absolutism' exhibited in the works of Aristotle and Kant. Definitive of categorial relativism is the belief that the categories involved in our thought and talk about reality might well be replaced by alternative categories, since thought and talk about reality might change in such a fundamental way. It would not follow that categorial description could not be true, simply that a true categorial description would not be unrevisable in consequence of a fundamental change in the way in which reality is thought and talked about. Categorial absolutism, on the other hand, does not envisage the revisability of the fruits of categorial enquiry.

Aristotle and Kant were categorial absolutists for different reasons. The reason for Aristotle is not difficult to discern. As categories are the natural, real divisions which reality itself exhibits then it is not surprising that the correct description of these categories will remain true for all time. Presumably our thought and talk about reality might not remain static, and might not always correctly reflect in its fundamental features the categories of reality discovered by Aristotle: how we would then be able to emulate Aristotle and discover them for ourselves is of course not obvious, but that is a difficulty which Aristotle's form of categorial absolutism would have to live with. Perhaps some way could be discovered of proving that the fundamental features of thought and talk could not themselves ever be different from what they are, since they reflect a reality which is itself unchanging.

Kant thought that he could prove that such features were unrevisable even though they did not so reflect reality, and that proof constitutes his grounds for categorial absolutism. In the better parts of the *Critique of Pure Reason* he seems to assume no more than that our thought has the features listed as the twelve categories just as our human perception is such as to place all perceived objects in a spatiotemporal framework. Other creatures might not share our space and time manner of perceiving things, and in the same way other creatures might not share our categorial divisions. When Kant writes like this he is adopting a form of categorial relativism: categorial description is relative to a certain kind of thought, and different categories might be exhibited by a different kind of thought about reality. But Kant frequently goes beyond such categorial tolerance and explicitly argues for the thesis that experience is not possible without the imposition of the twelve fundamental concepts listed as the twelve categories. Thus he argues, for example, in the section of the *Critique* called the 'Analytic of Principles', for the categories of substance, cause and reciprocity: any experience which, as *experience* must, makes room for objective time determinations – for the difference between 'This actually precedes that' and 'This is experienced before that' – must involve the categories of substance, cause and reciprocity.[6] Whether such a 'transcendental' proof of the categories can ever really establish the absolute status of such fundamental concepts, or forever remain open to the challenge to prove the inevitability of the other features of experience appealed to, is the inescapable problem for Kant's absolutism.

Of course, rejecting absolutism need not involve giving up appeal to some kind of transcendental argument in category description: only the argument will not establish the kind of conclusion hoped for by Kant himself. It would be a way of exhibiting the interconnections discernable between categories, and that is part of the task of categorial description.

Must a minimal form of categorial description adopt a positive stand, with Collingwood, against the categorial absolutist? I do not think so. Certainly a metaphysician describing the categories embedded in our thought and talk about reality need not make Collingwood's positive commitment to categorial change, rejecting the arguments and conclusions of various brands of categorial absolutism. Moreover it is not necessary even to adopt relativism as a methodological principle in order to engage in the minimal metaphysical pursuit, making a positive practical assumption that things might be other than they are. All that is needed is the kind of response shown before to categorial realism.

In a word, the minimal metaphysical enterprise of categorial description, which I am introducing, seeks to spell out the fundamental features of our thought and talk about reality, assuming *neither* the adequacy or otherwise of such categories to reality in itself *nor* the fixed or changing nature of that thought and talk.

4. *Strawson on description versus prescription*
My approach to metaphysics as an exercise in categorial description owes more than a little to Strawson's *Individuals*, but there is much in that work's distinction between descriptive

and revisionary metaphysics which I disagree with. Take, to begin with, the manner in which Strawson contrasts these two activities:

> Descriptive metaphysics is content to describe the actual structure of our thought about the world, revisionary metaphysics is concerned to produce a better structure. . . . Perhaps no actual metaphysician has ever been, both in intention and effect, wholly the one thing or the other. But we can distinguish broadly: Descartes, Leibniz, Berkeley are revisionary, Aristotle and Kant descriptive.[7]

I think it is a substantial criticism of this characterisation that the philosophers mentioned did not see themselves in these terms, and would have given a very different account of their intentions. Kant comes closest to Strawson's account of him though he would have much to say about why the structure of our thought is the only legitimate quarry. The rest would not recognise themselves in Strawson's characterisation. They did not see themselves as primarily involved with an account of thought at all, but with an account of reality. Certainly they often quite consciously concentrated on reality indirectly through an a priori study of the nature of our understanding, thought or knowledge: but such is the nature of a rationalist enquiry into reality. These philosophers were, in the terminology adopted above, realist metaphysicians.

There is reason to hesitate too over Strawson's way of characterising descriptive metaphysics, for one thing since in his programmatic comments he divides off thought and language from one another. Descriptive metaphysics, he says, concerns the most general features of our conceptual structure, and although

> . . . up to a point, the reliance upon a close examination of the actual use of words is the best, and indeed the only sure, way in philosophy . . . when we ask how we use this or that expression, our answers, however revealing at a certain level, are apt to assume, and not to expose, those general elements of structure which the metaphysician wants revealed.[8]

I have spoken of categorial description as concerning the fundamental features of our *thought* and *talk* about reality, assuming a major degree of matching between thought and talk. We can, if we like, treat thought as the primary quarry and talk as a way of approaching it: but to abandon this connection and try to approach thought without concentrating (*inter alia*) on features of language is like trying to study somebody's character whilst ignoring his behaviour. For how else can we get at our subject matter? Certainly the peculiar and seductive method of transcendental argument adopted by Strawson from Kant is notoriously ineffective, since it allows at most a proof that *if* our conceptual scheme has such-and-such features *then* it must have so-and-so others. But how do we know whether it has such-and-such in the first place? We cannot abandon language altogether.

Moreover, Strawson takes descriptive metaphysics to concern itself with the *unchanging* fundamental features of thought, and it is clearly contentious that there are any such features. He writes:

> There is a massive central core of human thinking that has no history – or none recorded in histories of thought; there are categories and concepts which, in their most fundamental character, change not at all. . . . They are the commonplaces of the least refined thinking; and are yet the indispensable core of the conceptual equipment of the most sophisticated human beings. It is with these, their interconnections, and the structure that they form, that a descriptive metaphysics will be primarily concerned.[9]

Now the kind of thing Strawson has in mind are such conceptual devices as a material object, the spatiotemporal framework of things, and persons. But is it not now a commonplace (though not of course for that reason true) to mark, say, the fundamental difference between a Greek teleological notion of matter and the inert substance of our post-Renaissance culture? Is it uncontentious that all peoples at all times share fundamentally the same notion of time and space? Do peoples with such notions as fate and demonic spiritual forces have the same idea of causation as twentieth-century Europeans? And would it not make a great difference to our notion of a person if we shared the Hindu belief in Karma and the rebirth of the individual? Or, when we compare different legal and moral codes, do we find a common factor which is an unchanging concept of a person?

Strawson shares with Kant and Aristotle what I have called an absolutist approach in metaphysics, closely connected with this belief in the unchanging nature of our thought structure. Though he makes frequent references to descriptive metaphysics' concern with 'our actual structure of thought', with 'our conceptual scheme as it is', the direction of his arguments frequently looks like a rejection of the idea of any alternatives to our scheme being in any way viable. In Chapter 2 of *Individuals*, for instance, where the question at issue is whether a conceptual scheme which involves the identification and reidentification of particulars must involve spatial notions too, the conclusion is drawn that this must indeed be so. Any conceptual scheme which has particulars figuring in it is of necessity one in which spatial relations figure – a powerful conclusion of surprising generality. Further, in Chapter 3, he rejects alternative notions of a person not (as we might expect) because they are inadequate descriptions of our concept of a person but because they are internally incoherent: our notion of a person is the only viable one since it is the only one passing the test of coherence. It is not surprising from Strawson's point of view that our conceptual machinery has no history, since there are no alternatives to it. In our previous terminology, Strawson is in this mood advocating an absolutist metaphysics. But, paradoxically, if our only tool for discovering metaphysical truth is the transcendental argument it is hard to see how metaphysics can be anything else.

5. *Categories as fundamental kinds*
It might be thought that Strawson's thesis of unchanging and unrevisable categories shared by all peoples at all times is not open to refutation from the above examples, since they are not actually categories at all. The point is that my examples might not look to be as fundamental, general, basic or ultimate as Strawson's, and hence are not the fundamental features of conceptual schemes. They are not, therefore, categories. But

the point stands, even if the argument must then be revised, that it is not at all *obvious* that there are no alternatives to the particular categories which we use in our thought and talk. If it is true that only one set of categories is possible for us that is a matter of substantial importance, and it would need to be specifically and carefully argued for.

A question is suggested by this rebuttal of my criticism, though, which is of general relevance for what follows. Is fundamentality an all-or-nothing affair, or are there simply degrees of it? I suppose, in the abstract, the answer is both; since we can conceive of the series of greater degrees of fundamentality ending, at least for some series, in a most fundamental. With specific reference to categories, however, to assume that there is a set of most fundamental concepts is perhaps to assume too much. Certainly it is to assume more than we are at present able to show. Moreover, maybe on some given criterion of fundamentality it is obvious that the concept of substance is less fundamental than the concept of a subject of discourse, or the concept of a cause is less fundamental than that of a ground or source; maybe, though, other criteria will suggest themselves in terms of which this is not so. It cannot be readily assumed that one and only one method of classification of concepts reveals the truth about fundamentality relations, and it is better to begin by looking, not for the *most* fundamental concepts in our conceptual scheme, but for the *more* fundamental. Categories can be thought of as these more fundamental features of our thought and talk about reality.

Once identified and described, it can then be asked whether some of these are indeed even more fundamental than the rest and criteria for deciding the issue will then have to be carefully specified. And another issue will need at the same time to be clarified, namely the consequences of any interdefinability of the favoured candidates for categorial status. At first glance, it seems fairly obvious that the concept of a substance or particular is intimately related to those of a property and a place, to name just a few. Kant's system of twelve categories is a case in point, since it was supposed to be a system of the twelve mutually independent but collectively exhaustive fundamental concepts.[10] In other words, all twelve categories listed were supposed to be independent concepts and all twelve were needed to provide a complete listing of the fundamental features of thought. Now the list of twelve logical forms of judgement from which the categories were derived is in fact open to criticism along these dimensions, since on the one hand it is clear that some of the forms are definable in terms of others, and on the other hand not all logical forms of judgement which we now recognise are included in the list. And what, after all, is the category of reciprocal interaction if not the joint categories of substance and cause?

In sum, if categorial status is reserved solely for the *most* fundamental features of our conceptual scheme it looks as though we might end up with very few categories indeed, and set ourselves a very difficult task right at the start. If we see categorial description as involved with the *more* fundamental features, at least in the beginning of our researches, we can hope for a richer landscape to depict.

II. METAPHYSICS IN PHILOSOPHY

By identifying an activity of categorial description I do not wish to imply that metaphysics can be pursued in total isolation from other branches of philosophy such as epistemology or the philosophy of mind. Indeed, quite the opposite is the case since the problems of philosophy are fundamentally interconnected. I will illustrate this point with two examples, since it is of real importance for understanding the place of metaphysics in philosophy as a whole, and because it tends to be masked by the need to divide up philosophy in undergraduate courses. My first example will be Descartes' famous attempted proof of the dual nature of a person, and my second example will be the problem of the ontological status of facts. Both of these also provide illustrations of categorial description, albeit in Descartes' case of a realist metaphysical persuasion.

1. Descartes on mind and body
Descartes devotes a good deal of his *Meditations on First Philosophy*[11] to the nature of persons, but it is easy enough briefly to spell out the major argument in support of his dualism of mind and body. In the hope of establishing an unassailable

body of philosophical and scientific knowledge he explicitly adopts a policy of withholding assent 'no less carefully from what is not plainly certain and indubitable than from what is obviously false', sweeping away the whole of what he has inherited from others as so-called knowledge or acquired through his own senses or reason. By the beginning of the Second Meditation, however, he thinks he has discovered one thing which he cannot doubt, namely that he exists. 'This proposition "I am", "I exist", whenever I utter or conceive it in my mind, is necessarily true.'[12] He then reasons as follows:

1. I can be certain that I exist.
2. I cannot be certain that I have a body.
So 3. My existence does not involve a body.
So 4. I exist as a thinking thing, a *res cogitans*.

Faced with this argument on its own one must obviously assume that Descartes is trying to prove that he, the referent of the 'I' in the argument, is a mind and nothing else; and that is not at all the same thing as saying that persons are a combination of two substances. But Descartes does actually intend to offer, in the Sixth Meditation, a proof of the existence of bodies also and so complete his argument for dualism. His preoccupation in the argument before us is to establish the distinction between mind and body, which leaves open the possibility of the existence of the one without the other and so provides the basis for his dualism. We might say that his intention is to establish his existence as at least a thinking substance, a thing which could conceivably have an existence even if no body were conjoined to it.

As for the validity of the argument and the grounds for its premisses we need not question too carefully. The first premiss which I have identified emerges from his attempt at doubting quite literally everything, and premiss 2 he thinks he has established by sceptical arguments concerning the senses and reason. The validity of the move from 3 to 4 rests of course on just what is contained in the word 'thing' and exactly what is implied by the notion of a thinking thing, a substance whose very essence is thought. 'What is that? A being that doubts, understands, asserts, denies, is willing, is unwilling; further that has sense and imagination.' One has only to reflect that conclusion 4 implies that if Descartes were ever to stop thinking for a moment (perhaps in dreamless sleep) he would go out of existence, to see that 4 is quite a jump to take from 3.

Our interest in the argument really centres on the move from premises 1 and 2 to the intermediate conclusion 3. Bernard Williams, in his book *Descartes: The Project of Pure Enquiry*, points out that this argument 'uncomfortably resembles a fallacy recognised by Stoic logicians, which came to be known as the *larvatus* or "masked man" fallacy: I do not know the identity of this masked man; I do know the identity of my father; therefore this masked man is not my father.'[13] Descartes' own contemporaries were quick to point this out also, and in particular the French philosopher Antoine Arnauld objected to Descartes' trying to prove something about the nature of reality (the nature of a person) from subjective premises about what he is and what he is not certain of.

Now in Descartes' defence we can surely ask whether premises 1 and 2 are simply subjective claims about Descartes himself, since he has taken great pains to argue in their support. What they propose is not simply the fact that he is certain about one thing and not certain about something else, but that he *can* be certain about the one and *cannot* be certain about the other – and both for perfectly logical reasons. However that may be, we can also come to his defence by pointing out that the procedural rule which he adopted at the beginning of the *Meditations*[14] lends considerable support to the argument in allowing the move from 2 to another conclusion 3a 'I can reject it as false, just as if I had overwhelming evidence to that effect, that I have a body', and that goes some way to establishing the required conclusion 3.

But the important thing for us to note is the way that a question about the nature of things, and therefore an issue concerning categorial description, is intimately tied up in Descartes' reasoning with questions about what we can or cannot be certain of, an issue in epistemology. And the same emerges from a brief perusal of a second version of the argument which is offered by Descartes in the Sixth Meditation.

Here he moves to his required conclusion, that the mind and

the body are two distinct substances, by means of a premiss concerning the power of God. By that point in the *Meditations* he thinks he has proved God's existence, so that is now available to him to figure in the argument as a new consideration. The argument goes as follows:

1. I can conceive of myself existing without a body.
2. God can make actual what I can conceive as possible.
So 3. The mind and the body can exist without each other.
So 4. There is a real distinction between mind and body.

In his own words, 'I know that whatever I clearly and distinctly understand can be made by God just as I understand it; so my ability to understand one thing clearly and distinctly apart from another is enough to assure me that they are distinct, because God at least can separate them'.[15] And again, in *The Principles of Philosophy* he writes that

> Each of us conceives of himself as a conscious being, and can in thought exclude from himself any other substance, whether conscious or extended; so from this mere fact it is certain that each of us, so regarded, is really distinct from every other conscious substance and from every corporeal substance. . . . For however closely [God] had united them, he could not deprive himself of his original power to separate them, or to keep one in being without the other; and things that can be separated, or kept in being separately, by God are really distinct.[16]

Premiss 1 is established by the same reasoning as before, that is by considerations about what Descartes can be certain of, and therefore involves epistemological issues. The conclusion, that mind and body are distinct substances, is the metaphysical conclusion reached before. Once more, a close connection between metaphysical and epistemological issues is evident.

2. Ontological status of facts
I now move on to my second example, the problem of the ontological status of facts. A fact is a peculiar sort of thing, a special kind of being, the peculiarity of which is a prime target

for categorial description. Though it figures neither in Aristotle's list of the predicables nor in Kant's list of pure concepts of the understanding, it is not difficult to see that the activity of comparing and contrasting facts with other sorts of being is closely related to the justifications which might be given for the lists of Aristotle and Kant. As categorial description concerns the fundamental types of things for which our conceptual scheme makes provision it needs little argument to show that facts should figure in such an activity just as much as particulars, properties and events.

Napoleon is a particular being, a thing which might be called a substance, and so are Big Ben, Ben Nevis and my desk. All these things have from one point of view a claim to be called particulars even though there are obvious differences between them. They all fall under the category of particular, having an existence as substances standing in various relations to one another. But facts are very different from particulars. It is a fact that Napoleon met his Waterloo, that my desk is made of wood, and that Ben Nevis is taller than Big Ben. Though these facts all involve particulars they cannot be equated with those particulars or treated as particulars in their own right. And, moreover, not all facts involve particulars – witness the fact that being blue is being coloured.

That they cannot be equated with those particulars is clear enough, since both Ben Nevis and Big Ben figure in the above fact; and they figure of course in similar facts concerning all other particulars too. That facts are not themselves particulars follows from the point that whereas particulars can be dated and located, facts cannot. When and where is the fact that being blue is being coloured? When and where is the fact that if my desk had not been made of wood it would have been made of metal? When and where, indeed, is the fact that Napoleon met his Waterloo – at Waterloo in 1815? Surely not, since it *is* a fact that Napoleon met his Waterloo even today, and no matter where I am putting it down on paper.

Actually, this point can be argued most easily by instancing facts which are about non-spatiotemporal phenomena or phenomena which exist through all space and all time. When and where, for example, would we place the fact that $2 + 2 = 4$ and the fact that 2 is an even number? When and where would we place the fact that the gravitational attraction between any two bodies varies with the distance between them? When and where the fact that if the temperature of a fermenting must rises much above 32°C the yeast cells cease producing alcohol? But the case is the same with facts about happenings that can be dated and located, such as Napoleon meeting his Waterloo.

A possible objection to this is that the fact that Napoleon met his Waterloo is datable to the extent that it was not so *before* 1815: it has been a fact *since* then, we might say. On the other hand we can say (with hindsight) that before 1815 it was a fact that Napoleon would meet his Waterloo and the relationship between that fact and the present one is not very perspicuous. Perhaps we should equate the two, and conclude that the (single) fact had no beginning in 1815. Alternatively we might distinguish the two by saying that it is a fact that before 1815 Napoleon was going to meet his Waterloo and it is a fact that since 1815 Napoleon has met his Waterloo: and these facts had no beginning and will have no end. The problem arises, if at all, only with a subclass of facts, those concerning spatiotemporally locatable happenings, events or processes. The general truth seems to be that facts are not themselves spatiotemporal beings, and the problematic cases can most easily be subsumed under this truth too. We do not think and talk of facts as we do of particulars.

Further evidence can be drawn from the possibility of facts of more complex kinds than the examples already given, such as the fact that Napoleon did not meet his Waterloo in 1810, the fact that my desk is not made out of metal, and the fact that if this desk were made out of metal it would not be my desk. Finding a time and a place for such interesting facts would be labour indeed.

Nor do we talk or think of facts as we do of happenings and of properties. The same reasoning as above establishes this point for happenings, since they as well as particulars are spatiotemporal beings. We can divide happenings into those that (relatively speaking) take place at a moment and are called events and those that take place over a longer period and are called processes. Events can be located at their moment of being and processes by giving the beginning and end points of their duration. Moreover happenings of both kinds are locatable in space, either (relatively speaking) at a place or spread over an area of space. Napoleon meeting his Waterloo happened in 1815 and at Waterloo, and my desk being made out of wood (the actual constructing of it) took rather longer and happened in a certain factory in England. As all happenings have this spatiotemporal locatability we can conclude that facts are not happenings, neither events nor processes. That facts are not properties needs a different argument, however, since properties are not so obviously spatiotemporal either.

But properties have the peculiarity that we distinguish between a property 'in itself' and the same property 'of a particular': we talk of redness in itself and of the redness of this jacket. Now redness in itself is a being which cannot be spatiotemporally located, no more than, say, justice or equality to two right-angles. The redness of this jacket, however, is the kind of thing which can be given spatiotemporal location since it exists as long as this jacket is red and is in the same place as the jacket. The fact that this jacket is red is not then to be equated with the redness of the jacket. And quite independently of this consideration is the point that properties are things that are possessed by particulars whereas facts are not. The redness of the jacket is a property of the jacket, and hence 'belongs to' or 'is had by' the jacket. The fact that the jacket is red is a fact about the jacket but not possessed by the jacket. We do not talk or think of facts in the way we do of properties.

Despairing of finding some type of entity in the world itself with which to equate facts, some philosophers have tried equating them with propositions – or rather, with *true* propositions, since false propositions do not seem to be closely associated with facts in the same way. But this is a mistake. Facts are rather what *make* true propositions true; a proposition is true *because* of the facts. It is true to say that Ben Nevis is taller than Big Ben since it is a fact that Ben Nevis is taller than Big Ben. The latter makes the former true. The conclusion to be drawn is that fact, particular, event, property, and proposition all are different categories of being.[17]

For our purposes, it is necessary to note the implications of this discovery for the relationship between metaphysics and other philosophical enterprises. The most relevant point is that facts are not to be equated with any spatiotemporal existents in the world: particulars, events, processes, and properties of these entities all have spatiotemporal location, and facts do not. That is not to say that facts are not themselves entities 'in the world', since why assume that reality is coextensive with spatiotemporal existents? It is, however, enough to leave open certain possibilities which might otherwise be closed. Take moral philosophy, for example.

It has long been reasoned that an unbridgeable distinction should be recognised between fact and value, since values are not to be equated with any spatiotemporal existents. In Moore's terminology values are 'non-natural' properties not to be equated with anything spatiotemporal, without committing the 'naturalistic fallacy'.[18] That someone or something is good or bad, or an act right or wrong, is somehow peculiarly unlike the constituents of the natural world. But there is a fallacy involved in this reasoning, and in any philosophical position like Moore's which removes value from reality as such and that fallacy should be obvious. Admit if you like that moral facts are not quite the same as facts about spatiotemporal phenomena such as Tabby being on the sofa, but do not for that reason deny moral facts a place in reality at all. Facts are not themselves spatiotemporal existents, and this is true even of facts *about* spatiotemporal existents. And moral values may therefore also be allowed to be matters of fact; it may also be allowed that moral facts have a place in reality.

The existence of facts does not directly presuppose the existence of the spatiotemporal world, except insofar as they are facts about such a world. The existence of facts presupposes a manner of establishing them, criteria for deciding what the facts are, and only since that itself presupposes people to make such decisions and adopt such criteria does the existence of the spatiotemporal world become itself implied. And if there are criteria for making decisions on matters of moral value it follows that the ground is laid for moral facts to enjoy existence. The same, indeed, is true of aesthetic facts.

So metaphysics has a close connection with issues in moral philosophy and in aesthetics. Even more obvious is its connection in this area with epistemology. The primary target of investigation in that field is the nature of knowledge, and knowledge implies (almost) uncontentiously the truth of that which is known. Any investigation of the nature of truth immediately comes up against the problem of the ontological status of facts, and their relation to diverse other things. It has often been pointed out that the empiricists' favourite theory of truth, the correspondence theory, according to which truth is a matter of correspondence between judgement and fact in the world, presupposes the locatability of the later in the spatiotemporal mind-independent reality of particulars, events, processes and so on. A decision on such a theory clearly depends on the categorial description of facts.

III. METAPHYSICAL CLAIMS: CRITERIA AND STATUS

1. Criteria are various
My primary purpose in this book is to introduce a kind of metaphysical pursuit which I have called a minimal activity, the activity of categorial description. Such an activity can be engaged in without assuming that the categories being depicted have any special unreplaceable status in our thought and talk about reality, and without assuming that they match or fail to match with features of reality existing independently of them. These assumptions, whatever can be said for them, are not needed to engage in categorial enquiry. What such an enquiry leads to is the depiction of the fundamental, categorial facts about our thought and talk.

I have just now said that facts exist insofar as there is a manner of establishing them, a criterion or some criteria in terms of which things can be judged to be as they are. Categorial facts depend therefore on such criteria too, but what are they? It is certainly not helpful to say that one judges categorial claims in terms of what is the case concerning our categories, since that is exactly what is at stake. It is more helpful to say that categorial claims are judged in terms of our *talk* about reality, since this at least stresses the point argued above about the connection between thought and talk. And our *talk* about reality can itself be established by asking ourselves whether we would say so-and-so, or such-and-such – witness our discussion above on the distinction between facts and particulars. But there is something unsatisfactory about leaving our results in terms of a series of notes concerning what we would or would not say, though they doubtless would indicate quite a lot of things about our categories.

It would just *be* a lot of things, in that case. What we want is a more coherent, systematic account of the relation between our categories and between categories and derivative concepts. And so we have to go beyond a piecemeal description of thought and talk to spell out broad and sometimes only roughly correct approximations which overlook finer distinctions. Taken in the right spirit this can be seen as giving a part of the truth, rather than falsehood, and we can hope to fill out the details later without losing much of the substance of the broader strokes. After all, as Searle has said, without abstraction and idealisation there is no systematisation. Broad description in natural science ignores much of the finer features of reality, but achieves a deeper understanding for all that.

Moreover, we must expect metaphysics' relation with other philosophical enterprises to dictate to some extent the kind of description that has some point. It would not be out of place to talk in this connection of the philosophical helpfulness, the explanatory scope and strength, of particular categorial descriptions, and here again witness the description that I gave of facts. Against the background of past mistakes in moral philosophy, epistemology and so forth, such categorial description has achieved major relevance: in the philosophy of science, against a historical background of too simplistic an appreciation of the relationship between fact and theory, such a categorial description has achieved a very central place in current research. We will see, also, that categorial description is given point by certain mistakes currently being made in the expectation of giving greater clarity to our thought and talk about reality in the new 'essentialist metaphysics' of such as Kripke and Lewis.

2. Relativism, objectivity, cognitivism
If we wish to go beyond mere categorial description and profess knowledge of reality itself, I think categorial description still

has a place as a preliminary move in that larger pursuit. But one reason for adopting the minimal activity of category description was to avoid making the kind of substantial metaphysical claim favoured by philosophers in the past, and which has come under fire for lacking cognitive status and therefore being nonsensical. Without doubt, categorial descriptions have a perfectly valid claim to escape that kind of attack, since they constitute a depiction of the broader, more fundamental features of our activity of thinking and talking and are cognitively as little problematic as a depiction of the natural world in general. We may have problems in understanding how to fit into a general account of nature the intentional phenomena of thought and language, but such phenomena there are, and descriptions of them have as much right to cognitive status as the products of natural science. Categorial descriptions are meaningful and factual, and therefore philosophically unobjectionable. There is little mystery in the claim that particulars are a different kind of thing from properties.

But *are* there particulars and properties? Construed as a question about reality itself, rather than our thought and talk about reality, my official programme of categorial description excuses me from answering it: to attempt to do so would be to raise the truth of assumptions such as metaphysical absolutism and metaphysical realism. I will, nevertheless, take on these questions in my last chapter when the neutral stance of categorial description will be dropped. There I will try to show that categorial description is not in the final analysis a description of thought and talk simply, but of reality also. And I will try to show that the assumption of metaphysical absolutism is not at all required for that of metaphysical realism, since fact and objectivity are a consequence of a categorial framework such as our thought and talk adopts. Until that last chapter categorial description is the order of the day.

CHAPTER 2   SUBSTANCE

I. SUBSTANCES AS INDIVIDUAL OR PARTICULAR THINGS

Looking for some general terminology for the enterprise of categorial description, I have followed philosophical tradition and allowed the terms 'being', 'entity', 'existent' and 'thing' to designate variously the members of all categories. In this terminology it is as correct to call possibilities, necessities and pluralities 'things' etc. as it is to so call properties and particulars, and this without any implicit commitment to treating them all as the same *kind* of thing or giving them all the same *kind* of existence. But there is one very central category for which these words are undoubtedly specially apt and with which most of us would naturally associate them, namely the category of particular or individual things.

We normally contrast 'things' with their properties, the places and times in which they exist, the processes through which they evolve or in which they engage, the events that they take part in and so on; here we are making a special but quite commonplace use of the term, special indeed only in the sense that it limits its application more narrowly than the usage of the metaphysical specialist. A thing, in this narrow sense, is a particular entity or individual being, or a 'particular' or 'individual' for short.

A term favoured by metaphysicians as a variant on these is 'substance'. The category of substance, for as long as metaphysics has been engaged in, has attracted a great deal of attention – so much so that an account of the history of discussions of substance would virtually be one of metaphysics itself. I will provide no more than the briefest of such histories, but rather will move towards a general description of the category of substance as we have it embedded in our thought and talk about the world.

Metaphysicians have at least generally agreed in their use of the term 'substance' to refer to things which have independent existence, to which things happen and to which properties and relations can be attributed. Admittedly this is small enough agreement when the question of independent existence leaves great scope for varied opinions; but if we take it to refer to the way in which, say, Plato exists independently of Socrates but Plato's height does not exist independently of Plato himself we can adopt this agreed usage of the term as our own. Substances are the things about us in the world that have an independent existence and that have properties, stand in various relations to one another, and engage in events and processes.

I have already outlined Aristotle's way of identifying the category of substance, and as it is something I want to build on later I will now amplify it a little. Substances are for Aristotle, according to his general description of the categories, a special type of predicables, providing a class of answers to a special kind of question. In this they contrast with, say, attributes such as being tall or being old. To assign Socrates to the class of humans is to say what kind of individual or particular thing he is; a man is a kind of substance, in this terminology. On the other hand, being tall or old is a matter of having the attribute of tallness or old age, and ascribing such attributes to Socrates is not the same thing as saying of Socrates that he is a man. A man *is* a substance (particular) and *has* attributes such as tallness and old age.

In fact, Aristotle has another very different notion of substance as well, and we ought to be aware of its connection with and difference from this one: Aristotle himself distinguishes them as 'primary substance' and 'secondary substance'. It is quite easy to confuse the two since referring expessions such as 'a man' and 'water' happen to refer ambiguously to primary and secondary substances in Aristotle's sense of the terms. In the sentence 'A man walked into the room' the expression 'a man' is referring to a specific individual, an individual thing or primary substance; in the sentence 'A man is a featherless biped' it is referring to a kind or class, a species, or secondary substance. In the sentence 'Water filled the jar' the expression 'water' is referring to a specific sample of water, so a primary substance; while in the sentence 'Water is made of hydrogen and oxygen' the reference is to a kind of matter, hence to a secondary substance.

Aristotle himself marks the difference as follows in his *Categories*:

> A substance – that which is called a substance most strictly, primarily, and most of all – is that which is neither said of a subject nor in a subject, e.g. the individual man or the individual horse. The species in which the things primarily called substances are, are called secondary substances, as also are the genera of these species. For example, the individual man belongs in a species, man, and animal is a genus of the species; so these – both man and animal – are called secondary substances.[1]

For Aristotle, then, not only are there the primary substances which are particular, individual things, but there are secondary substances which are the species and genera – more briefly the kinds – into which these primary substances fall.

'A man', therefore, and 'water' too, can be used to refer either to primary substances or to secondary substances, that is to particular things and parcels of matter or to the kind or class to which these things belong. A failure to mark the distinction between those two referents is at the very least to confuse classes with their members.

Actually the term 'substance' in common parlance is closer to Aristotle's idea of secondary substance than primary. My dictionary includes this entry under the term: '*Substance* . . . particular kind of matter (a heavy, porous, yellow, transparent, [substance]; the small number of [substances] that make up the world'. We do say, of course, such things as that gold is a different substance from silver, indeed that wood is a different substance from plastic; and such use of the term is quite different from Aristotle's 'primary substance'. We seem rather to be referring to the classes from which individuals are drawn, the kinds rather than the individuals themselves.

The question before us in this chapter is the correct categorial description of the individual thing, hence of

Aristotle's primary substance. The complementary question concerning secondary substance will be dealt with, *inter alia*, in Chapter 3.

II. WHAT SUBSTANCES ARE NOT

1. Locke's substratum
Of the various accounts of substance propounded by philosophers probably the best known is the 'substratum' theory usually associated with John Locke. My dictionary in fact gives this as the philosophical meaning of the term: '*Substance*: (Metaphysics) the substratum that the cognisable properties or qualities or attributes or accidents of things are conceived as inhering in or affecting'. This is but one among many accounts, but prominent enough in philosophical history to merit first consideration.

Quite what was Locke's real attitude to the metaphysical thesis of substrata is very much open to question, and it is arguable that Locke was not propounding an account of what *he* thought substances to be but describing an idea which men in general think they have but which he believes to be fundamentally confused.[2] This interpretation would at least save him from the often quoted objection that the idea of substance is an inevitable stumbling block for an empiricist such as he was, and that accepting the validity of such an idea is simply being inconsistent with an empiricist stand. Locke's empiricism commits him to the position that the only ideas we possess are either derived directly from experience or built up by a process of simple accretion out of these directly derived ideas. The idea of a substratum of properties is not derived from experience directly, but nor is it a compound of such ideas, so it follows for an empiricist that there is no such idea. If Locke thought there was then he was no empiricist.

Locke describes the origin and nature of the idea of a substratum as follows, suggesting that the idea is *per impossibile* a consequence of reasoning or inference and that it has indeed no content:

> The mind . . . takes notice . . . that a certain number of these
> simple ideas go constantly together; . . . not imagining how
> these simple ideas can subsist by themselves, we accustom
> ourselves to suppose some substratum wherein they do
> subsist, and from which they do result; which therefore we
> call substance.[3]

Take, for example, this table. We notice a certain colour,
texture, set of shapes and so on constantly conjoined, which we
do not yet identify with 'the table'. Not being able to conceive
these simple properties as existing in themselves without
something to inhere in, we suppose they inhere in a substratum
which we add to those properties as an integral part of the table.
And as for the content of the idea of a substratum, it is a
'something, we know not what'. 'If anyone will examine himself
concerning his notion of pure substance in general, he will find
he has no other idea of it at all, but a supposition of he knows
not what support of such qualities.'[4]

Now Locke is introducing, in the idea of a substratum of
properties, an idea of 'pure substance in general', and if we ask
what account is implied of particulars we get the following: a
particular (such as this table, this glass of water, that tree) is
conceived of as a collection of properties which are supported
by a substratum. The substratum itself is conceived of as
propertyless, since it is what underlies the properties and in
which they subsist. Indeed, it would not be possible to point to
any difference between the substratum of this table and of this
glass of water, since without properties there can be no
differences. This fact alone should be sufficient to make us
pause, and ask what the Lockean thesis of a substratum is
doing. It is going to be no help in individuating one particular
from another, quite obviously, or in recognising a particular as
the same one which we previously encountered. Nor is it going
to help us in classifying particulars into their different kinds,
since the substratum is the same throughout particulars. At
best, perhaps, it will provide the bare foundation for an account
of change along the lines of the substratum losing some and
gaining other properties – but on the face of it, the substratum
being just the bare foundation of those properties, this account
will stop at that very starting point.

No, the answer is that the substratum thesis satisfies a demand set up by Locke's imagined argument: a particular has a number of distinguishable properties, which we observe collected together in the particular; properties cannot inhere in each other (the colour of the table cannot belong to the shape of the table, for example) and neither can they inhere in *nothing* (they must be properties of *something*); so there must be something which has these properties. For Locke, this something is the substratum.

There is a much more natural answer to this demand for a 'something' to have the properties – the particular itself, of course. It is the table itself which has its colour and shape, not some featureless substratum. But this is so obvious that it must be asked why Locke did not give this answer himself. Perhaps he thought that the alternative to equating a particular to its properties plus the substratum was equating it to its properties alone; so that taking properties to belong to particulars was effectively giving a reductive account of particulars. The table would then just be the properties which we have so far supposed it to have, its square shape, brown colour, smooth texture, rigidity of structure and so forth. But properties are not the kind of thing which can exist independently of something for them to be properties *of*, they must in other words be instantiated in some thing of a different nature, a particular which *has* the properties. Reducing particulars themselves to properties leaves nothing for properties to be possessed by, and so no possibility of their being instantiated. It makes nonsense both of the idea of particulars and the idea of properties.

If this line of thought was behind Locke's substratum theory, then he should not have been persuaded by it. True, the concepts of particular and property go hand in hand, properties being possessed by particulars, particulars possessing properties. That in itself however does not block a reductive analysis of particulars to groups of properties, since it is not at all obvious that a group, class or collection of properties is not itself anything over and above the properties themselves. In other words, the group could have peculiar features which are not possessed by the properties themselves, for example, and quite importantly a spatiotemporal location. Moreover, what would be grouped together in the particular table – rigidity, squareness, brownness and so on, or *its* rigidity, *its* squareness, *its* brownness? If there are reasons for saying the latter, then we have twice over reintroduced particularity in our reductive account, the particularity of spatiotemporal location and of the instantiation of properties.

There is however no need to take too seriously a reductive approach to particulars as the only alternative to the substratum theory. The major weakness of the imagined Lockean line of argument is the equation of the correct thesis that the particular table possesses its properties with that reductive thesis. To say that *the table* has the properties of being square, brown, rigid and so on is certainly to say that they do not belong to something else – a substratum – but neither is it to say that they belong to nothing, are simply a group of properties clustered together. It is precisely to say that they belong to or are instantiated by a particular, an individual which has a spatiotemporal location and stands in various relationships of a spatiotemporal and causal kind to other particulars. Particulars are what they are, not properties or classes of properties, and their peculiarity is to have this kind of relationship to properties. They cannot be reduced to what they are not.

2. *Empiricists' objects*

Modern empiricism has inherited much from John Locke, and his substratum thesis finds its correlate in the twentieth-century theory of logical atomism. In fact, Wittgenstein's *Tractatus* offers a theory of 'objects' which (at least on one interpretation) are as featureless as the substrata of Locke.[5] 'In a manner of speaking, objects are colourless' writes Wittgenstein, expressing in his usual cryptic style the idea that the properties of the world with which we are conversant are the consequences of the ways in which 'objects' come together to form structures. One might almost think he is talking about the subatomic particles of modern physics, and clearly there is at least a broad analogy between that and logical atomism, but there are many reasons for not equating the two. After all, modern physics does ascribe various differentiating properties to its particles.

Wittgenstein's theory is a logical, not a physical, one and

defended on a priori grounds. The objects of the theory are said to be featureless constituents of 'states of affairs'; these states of affairs are the product of the structural relationships between objects, and are equivalent to particulars at the 'macro' level having properties and standing in various relationships to one another. Wittgenstein's objects are further said to be indestructible, since they form 'the substance of the world'. States of affairs come and go, objects go on for ever.

The existence of these objects is put forward on a priori grounds, and even though Wittgenstein can neither point to an object nor give us any identifying description of one – either act requiring that objects *per impossibile* have features – he thinks he can prove their existence. The comments I made about Locke's substrata appear just as apt in relation to Wittgenstein's objects. Objects are going to provide no assistance in individuating one particular from another, at the level of ordinary macro particulars, nor in recognising a particular as the same one previously encountered. Neither will they help in classifying particulars into their different kinds, since they are by hypothesis the same throughout – at best, help in this direction would come from structures. And though Wittgenstein's thesis provides for an account of change along the lines of the restructuring of objects it offers little hope for further enrichment of that account. If the theory of objects has any positive merits it must be aimed at solving problems other than these.

Perhaps comparing logical atomism to physical atomism is misleading, in that it might suggest that the relationship between an ordinary particular such as a table and Wittgenstein's objects is that the former is simply made up of the latter in the way it is made up of atoms. The real flavour of the theory, and the basic consideration offered by Wittgenstein in its support, comes from shifting attention away from objects to their correlates in language, 'logically proper names'. Though there are other arguments discernable in the *Tractatus* for the existence of objects the major one turns on the explanation offered by Wittgenstein of the fact that sentences have meaning, i.e. can convey propositions. That is really the central concern of the book, even though the theory of objects is presented before the theory of meaning – or rather, before it is made obvious that it is functioning as part of a theory of meaning.

The explanation Wittgenstein gives of sentence meaning is that sentences are essentially reconstructions of the states of affairs which they are used to say exist. The sentence 'Tabby is on the sofa' says what it does by that sentence recreating the situation of Tabby's being on the sofa. If that is not obviously true, it is because 'language disguises thought' and the grammatical form of the sentence is misleading as to its true logical form. Any ordinary sentence such as this is actually a very complex compound of what Wittgenstein calls 'elementary propositions', and it is only these latter which are directly and undisguisedly models or pictures of states of affairs. These elementary propositions are composed of logically proper names – or simply 'names', as Wittgenstein calls them – which have no descriptive content or sense, but simply stand for objects. The argument for objects is that language has meaning, meaning is a matter of modelling or picturing reality, and this 'picture theory' implies the existence of logically proper names and so the existence of objects too.

Should we then accept this theory that individual things, particulars or substances of the kind we are directly conversant with in the world, are in this complicated fashion – *via* the complex structure of sentences about those particulars – manifestations of Wittgenstein's objects? And should we perhaps go even further and come to treat those objects as in some sense the *primary* or *basic* particulars, since it is out of them that ordinary particulars arise, and they are supposed to have many of the features usually ascribed to the latter: they are distinct existents, even though supposed not to be capable of independently existing out of combination with others; they do stand in relation to one another; they underlie the changes of states of affairs and persist through such events and processes.

To answer the easier question first, whether objects are more basic than ordinary particulars, it should be said that Wittgenstein apparently intended no more significance to be attached to their position as terminating the analysis of sentences than the role which the theory of meaning awards them. There is no intention to treat everyday particulars as in some way 'simply' manifestations of 'real' objects; that is,

Wittgenstein is not obviously committed to treating particular tables and chairs as no more than 'logical constructions' out of objects, if that means (as it did for Russell) that they are therefore taken to be unreal. If 'basic' implies only a fundamental role in giving language meaning, then objects are basic compared to tables.

The more difficult question asks us to pass judgement on the whole theory of meaning presented in the *Tractatus*, the picture theory. Well, there are many reservations we can register about that theory, some of which were developed by Wittgenstein himself in his later works such as the *Philosophical Investigations*, and the general consensus is that the theory must go. For one thing it offers at best an account of the meaning of fact-stating discourse, leaving out all sorts of interesting uses of language such as legal, moral, religious and philosophical. Indeed it implies the very meaninglessness of itself, since the a priori philosophical use of language is not a fact-stating one. Moreover it is clearly motivated by a referential approach to meaning – the meaning of sentences is explained by the reference of logically proper names to objects – and many philosophers (though by no means all) would now reject such an approach. For these reasons and others the peculiar argument of the *Tractatus* for objects is held to be unacceptable.

But more to the point from our interest in categorial description, we should note that Wittgenstein's objects do not, after all, satisfy some of the most central demands our conceptual scheme makes of particular things, even though they satisfy others. Features of particulars which do not belong to objects include the following: the fact that particular things enjoy independent existence; that they stand in such interesting relations to one another as spatial and temporal relations, and of course causal ones too; that they themselves undergo changes and take part in events and processes; and, most fundamentally, that they have properties, they serve as the means by which properties are instantiated – properties are properties *of* particulars, and particulars provide particular instantiations of properties. Objects have none of these features.

This consideration proves only that Wittgenstein's objects are themselves poor exemplars of our category of particular things, but not yet that they provide no part of the content of that category. After all, it is at least theoretically possible that our category of a particular thing finds instantiation in the ordinary macro particulars of the world only *via* some analogous but diminished concept of substance finding instantiation in more esoteric particulars such as Wittgenstein's objects. I think the most that could be claimed, even were we to accept the picture theory, would be that our concept of a particular is applicable only because Wittgenstein's concept of an object is applicable, since the applicability of the later concept is in the complex way demanded by the picture theory a precondition of our having and using *any concept whatsoever*. There is no direct relationship between the two concepts of substance such that it could possibly be claimed that the latter is part of the content of the former. Spelling out the content of the category of particular things is, in other words, possible without reference directly to Wittgenstein's objects, even on the assumption of the picture theory. And as that theory is not to be assumed anyway, as a discredited hypothesis to account for the meaning of language, we can safely conclude that our category of substance has no dependence on Wittgenstein's objects.

The other major proponent of logical atomism was Bertrand Russell, whose version of the theory was, in contrast to Wittgenstein's, heavily reductionist and propounded in the context of different philosophical preoccupations.[6] Russell was essentially involved with the fundamental question of epistemology – what do we know for certain? – rather than the question of language meaning, and sought to give an account of our thought and talk about the world which assumed the existence of the least number of different kinds of things and states of affairs. Occam's Razor, which requires entities not to be multiplied without necessity, for Russell was a counsel to make the least number of assumptions about existence in construing our beliefs about reality. The analysis of complex ordinary sentences into compounds of elementary propositions is still there, and so are logically proper names as (at least some of) the constituents of such propositions. The notion of a logically proper name is indeed Russell's invention, meaning a word which is really, or from a logical point of view, a name. 'A name is a simple symbol, directly designating an individual which is its meaning, and having this meaning in its own right, independently of the meanings of all other words', he writes.[7] Clearly 'John Smith' is not a logically proper name.

But then Russell has almost as much difficulty as Wittgenstein in giving any example of one: the best he can offer is 'this' or 'that', as applied to the immediate data of perception, sensedata such as a white patch in the visual field. Unlike Wittgenstein, he is happy to equate the referents of names with sensedata, and offers in effect a version of phenomenalism having much in common with David Hume's account of the particulars of the world. Russell's phenomenalism is, however, a linguistic one. Particulars such as tables and chairs are not *simply* collections of sensedata; rather sentences in ordinary language about particulars are analysable into sentences making reference, *via* logically proper names, to sensedata. For Russell this does mean that ordinary particulars are in a sense less basic than sensedata, in fact 'unreal', purely 'logical constructions' out of the latter. The things of the world are those fleeting objects of the private experiences of individual minds. And minds too are logical constructions out of sensedata.

I need not spell out in detail the extent to which sensedata fail to exemplify our category of particular or individual things, a concept which finds its paradigm application in the publicly available spatiotemporal objects in the causal world of tables, chairs, trees and so on. The only question we need address, even briefly, is whether Russell has given any account of a concept of a particular which is recognisedly ours. On the contrary, he has ignored the prior question of the content of our category of particulars in favour of the question of the analysis of sentences about such particulars which will satisfy the demands of Occam's Razor. It can hardly be said that that category itself implies the kind of analysis given of ordinary everyday particulars into sensedata, for that is the consequence of a desire to hedge one's bets about existence.

Before leaving these empiricists' approach to substance it is interesting to note that there are certain parallels to be discerned in the works of Leibniz, on all accounts a rationalist *par excellence*. Leibniz gives us two theories of substance, one of

which equates substances with entities he calls 'monads', the
other equating them with instantiations of 'complete notions'.
The theory of monads is a kind of atomism, more physical than
logical, which he thinks is supported by scientific discoveries
(some consequent on the invention of the microscope) as well as
a priori arguments. A monad 'is nothing but a simple substance
which enters into compounds; simple, that is to say, without
parts. . . . Now where there are no parts, there neither
extension, nor shape, nor divisibility is possible. And these
monads are the true atoms of nature and, in a word, the
elements of things'.[8] The *Monadology* goes on to develop various
interesting claims about these simple substances, such as their
indestructibility and inability to causally affect one another,
their activity as perceivers of all others of their kind and their
ability to rise above their present state to one closer to God.
Many of these claims remove monads from our category of
substance, putting them in this respect in the same position as
'objects' and sensedata.

The other theory of substance propounded by Leibniz seems
to take ordinary particulars into its scope as well as monads,
and construes all particulars as instantiations of complete
notions. 'It is very true that when several predicates are
attributed to one and the same subject, and this subject is not
attributed to any other, one calls this subject an individual
substance', he writes; but finding this Aristotelian account
'only nominal' he supplements it with the following:

> . . . it is the nature of an individual substance, or complete
> being, to have a notion so complete that it is sufficient to
> contain, and render deducible from itself, all the predicates
> of the subject to which this notion is attributed. On the other
> hand, an accident is a being whose notion does not include all
> that can be attributed to the subject to which this notion is
> attributed. . . . God, seeing the individual notion . . . of
> Alexander, sees in it at the same time the foundation of and
> reason for all the predicates which can truly be stated of him
> – as, for example, that he is the conqueror of Darius and
> Porus.[9]

This might at first sight seem quite acceptable. After all, is it
not the case that some set of facts about any individual will

exhaustively describe that individual, both its past and future as well as its present states? If so, that set of facts, true descriptions of the individual, could be said to be its 'complete notion'. But there is more to Leibniz's thesis than this.

What more can be seen from an implication which he draws from his thesis, namely that every true proposition about an individual substance is such that its predicate is contained in its subject – is 'analytic' as we would now say. If Alexander is the conqueror of Darius then the proposition stating that fact is analytic, since

> . . . when a proposition is not identical – that is, when the predicate is not contained expressly in the subject – it must be contained in it virtually. . . . The subject-term, therefore, must always include the predicate-term, in such a way that a man who understands the notion of the subject would also judge that the predicate belongs to it.[10]

But this creates havoc with our notion of a fact about an individual: on Leibniz's account, all such propositions are analytically true or necessarily false. If Alexander is referred to as 'the conqueror of Darius', then we would have less hesitation in accepting that saying Alexander conquered Darius was saying something analytic – 'The conqueror of Darius conquered Darius'. But referring to him simply as 'Alexander' allows the statement of this *contingent* truth about him. Leibniz is writing as though individual substances have a definition, which includes all truths about that individual, or worse still as though a name of an individual refers to such a complete definition of the individual. On the contrary, it refers to the individual.

3. Rigidly designated

It is a consequence of Leibniz's thesis, that particulars are the instantiations of complete notions, that all properties of particulars are contained in the subject terms introducing them into propositions. We want to say, however, that many properties of particulars are possessed by them purely contingently and Alexander conquering Darius is one such example. Indeed it is very tempting to say that all properties of particulars are contingently possessed, since it is difficult to see how any particular of the sort our category of substance picks out can have a property *of necessity*. Those peculiar entities called numbers apparently can – the number 7 is necessarily smaller than the number 8, and necessarily also odd rather than even; and we can make sense of properties themselves having other properties by definition – the property of being human necessarily implies the property of being a living thing, that of triangularity necessarily involves being rectilinear, and so on. We can make sense too of a particular having the properties which are consequent in this way on its being a member of a kind, but that must be distinguished from its having those properties non-contingently. For example, Alexander is a member of the class of humans, and this implies that he has the property of being a living thing; yet the only sense in which he has that property necessarily is that it is a necessary consequence of his being human, and what is more it is purely contingent that Alexander is a member of the class of humans.

We might conclude therefore that particulars have properties only contingently, had this thesis not been questioned recently by a number of philosophers, Saul Kripke being prominent amongst them.[11] Kripke argues that particulars have essential properties as well as contingent ones, and that this fact is reflected in our use of names to designate particulars. Names are said to be 'rigid designators' which refer to the *same* particulars in this world and in all possible worlds in virtue of their essential properties. In other words, a particular is rigidly designated by a name.

Putting forward his theory as an improvement on previous accounts of the way names function rather than explicitly as an account of particulars as such, Kripke has little difficulty in finding fault with the line adopted by Frege and Russell on ordinary names, that they are disguised descriptions. What is 'Alexander' a disguise of? If we say 'the conqueror of Darius' then it becomes, as we have seen, necessarily true that Alexander conquered Darius and that is indisputably at best a contingent truth. One might expect Kripke to try to improve on this line by taking names to be disguised descriptions where the descriptions are equivalent to the essential properties of the

things named, since then at least he would get the consequence
that all propositions asserting, of a named particular, its
essential properties come out necessarily true. If, for example,
Alexander were said (for the sake of argument) to be *necessarily*
the son of Philip of Macedon, then were 'Alexander' a disguised
version of 'the son of Philip of Macedon' it would turn out that
'Alexander was the son of Philip of Macedon' was necessarily
true, and that is just what Kripke wants.

But Kripke does not adopt this line. He insists, quite
plausibly, that names are not disguised descriptions at all, and
follows Mill in claiming them to be simple referring devices.
They designate what they designate without the aid of meaning
or connoting any property of the thing. The necessity linking
essential properties to their owners is not a reflection of the
meaning we assign to the names we use. Indeed, the essential
properties of a particular lie outside of our language use and
have to be discovered.

This seems to say that essential properties are after all
contingent, that if a particular necessarily has a property its
having that property is contingent, and that is self-
contradictory. The appearance of a contradiction is resolved by
drawing a distinction between epistemic necessity and
possibility on the one hand and the necessity and contingency
of property possession on the other. Kripke distinguishes
correctly between the a priori–a posteriori (empirical) distinction and the usual necessary-contingent distinction. It is
no part of the meaning of these terms that the distinctions are
either the same or totally match in their application, the same
in intension or extension. Kant thought that there could be
synthetic a priori truths, a possibility wholly unintelligible to
the empiricist tradition: Kripke goes even further and says
there are a posteriori necessary truths. Suppose 'Alexander'
rigidly designates Alexander in virtue of the essential property
of being the son of Philip of Macedon. Then it is a necessary
truth, since a necessary possession by Alexander of that
property, that Alexander is the son of Philip of Macedon, and
yet Kripke would hold that that would be something to be
discovered by us and so empirical. Until we knew its truth, it
would be epistemically possible that he did not have the
property, yet necessary that he did.

We can accept the theoretical possibility of such a category of truths without believing there are any examples. The onus is on Kripke to show that particulars do have essential properties, and this means that he must show that names do indeed rigidly designate particulars. To grasp the full import of this thesis we have to note the connection between the notion of a rigid designator and those of essential properties and possible worlds. Kripke is reintroducing, in this connection, Leibniz's idea of necessary truth being truth in all possible worlds. There are really two aspects to calling names rigid designators: firstly, they have no meaning, they connote no properties of what is designated; secondly, they designate the same particulars in all possible worlds, not just particulars in this world. How do they do this? Because particulars have certain properties which are essential to them, and therefore possessed in all possible worlds in which they exist as well as in the actual world. If Alexander has the essential property we have instanced then he has this property in *all* possible worlds – that is what is meant by an essential property.

Imagine a world in which things are different from ours *inter alia* in that someone with this property of Alexander had gone on to be a great philosopher, and his teacher in our world (Aristotle) had become the conqueror of all around him. Would we say that our name 'Alexander' designates in that world what 'Aristotle' designates in ours? Kripke says not. The name 'Alexander' is a rigid designator, rigidly designating Alexander in our world and hence designating the *same* individual – viz. the one having the same essential properties – in all possible worlds.

Kripke does not actually give this example of Alexander himself but I think it illustrates his thesis accurately. He gives few examples of essential properties, yet I think we might reasonably surmise that he has something like the actual parenthood of the individual in mind for people from his example of the impossibility of Queen Elizabeth II having been the daughter of Mr and Mrs Truman:

How could a person originating from different parents, from a totally different sperm and egg, be *this very woman*? One can imagine, *given* the woman, that various things in her life could have changed: that she could have become a pauper; that her royal blood should have been unknown, and so on. . . . But what is harder to imagine is her being born of different parents. It seems to me that anything coming from a different origin would not be this object.[12]

He says, similarly, of a particular wooden table that it could not have come from a totally different block of wood, or have been made of ice. There are no possible worlds in which *this* table has those properties, hence its having been made from one particular block of wood is an essential property of the table.

It is interesting to note that the identities of the Queen, Alexander and the table are being given in terms of those other individuals, and one might well wonder how, if at all, essential properties might be purely universal, general characteristics. Could not many individuals then share the essential properties, in this world or (more problematically) in different possible worlds? Would there not be a problem of saying which of Alexander's two doubles was Alexander in a possible world in which he has an identical twin? And if we are not clear on what we would say in that case, it suggests that *whatever* that would be it is not part of our use of the term 'Alexander' after all. Perhaps Kripke would take the line that all essential properties of individuals are uniquely possessed since they make essential use of other individuals themselves. Then the question becomes whether any individual can be imagined out of his actual life history, and if not then no Alexander can be postulated in any other possible world. So 'Alexander' would not be a rigid designator.

I think the fundamental objection to Kripke's account concerns the fact that our use of names is against the background of a socially shared appreciation of world history,[13] and though there are areas of ignorance where many things are indeed epistemically possible nevertheless we do have a great deal of knowledge of the contingent facts of the world and use our referential terms accordingly. What on earth we would say about what Alexander or Queen Elizabeth, or this table, could or could not do or be is a question which does not arise. What we would say about who was Alexander in an imaginary example of a possible world has little to do with our use of the name. As far as particulars are concerned, there do not seem to be any essential properties if they are meant to be the properties presupposed by our use of names. Our names designate individuals in the actual world.

But we do say 'Aristotle could have died before adulthood', and so *seem* to be designating the man in a world other than the actual one. That is an illusion. The word designates the man in this world – since there are no others – and the proposition asserts of him the contingency of his ever having become an adult.

The Kripkean thesis might be defended as at least offering an illuminating account of the way we talk about possibilities and impossibilities concerning particulars, by introducing the machinery of essential properties and possible worlds, on the grounds that these latter notions are clearer or easier to handle than such modal terms as 'must', 'could not' and so on. Kripke's terminology of possible worlds has in fact been a startlingly successful innovation, many philosophers seemingly finding his notions quite translucent and his thesis that names are rigid designators self-evidently true. We must be careful not to lose sight of the failure of this thesis to capture our actual use of names, however, even if we ultimately adopt it as a modification of our talk about particulars which is philosophically more transparent than present practice.

Yet Kripke himself seems to have justifiable doubts about this last supposed advantage, since he talks in the new preface to *Naming and Necessity* of the translatability of the possible world vocabulary *into* modal language:

> If one wishes to avoid the *Weltangst* and philosophical confusions that many philosophers have associated with the 'worlds' terminology, I recommend that 'possible state (or history) of the world', or 'counterfactual situation' might be better. One should even remind oneself that the 'world' terminology can often be replaced by modal talk – 'It is possible that . . .'.[14]

He even goes so far as to question the philosophical advantages of possible worlds in a footnote towards the end of that preface. He writes:

I do not think of 'possible worlds' as providing a *reductive* analysis in any philosophically significant sense, that is, as uncovering the ultimate nature, from either an epistemological or a metaphysical point of view, of modal operators, propositions, etc., or as 'explicating' them. . . . The main and the original motivation for the 'possible worlds analysis' – and the way it clarified modal logic – was that it enabled modal logic to be treated by the same set theoretic techniques of model theory that proved so successful when applied to extensional logic.[15]

III. WHAT SUBSTANCES ARE

To summarise, I have so far argued against certain claims made in the characterisation of Aristotle's primary substances, of the particular or individual things in the world about us. Firstly we saw that these particulars cannot be analysed into sets of properties plus a Lockean substratum, and saw reason to reject their analysis simply into sets of properties alone. Secondly, the theory propounded by more recent philosophers which treats particulars *via* the complex logical analysis of ordinary sentences as some kind of manifestation of simple objects or sensedata was also rejected. Leibniz's theories of substance were found wanting too, both his atomistic theory of monads and his equation of particulars with instantiations of complete notions. Finally, we have seen there are reasons enough to reject too the most recent approach to particulars as referents of rigid designators, with that theory's associated mechanism of possible worlds and essential properties. Things have not been all negative, however, since we have on the way been able to note some salient facts which do indeed pertain to particulars.

Particulars are, by common consent, independent existents. True, different interpretations have been put on such independence, some reading it so strictly that only one thing in the universe can be counted as a substance. Descartes thought God the only being capable of enjoying the position, and Spinoza was convinced it was God-or-nature, that is the universe itself. Less strict reading allows more things to share this status, and we can say that our category of particulars allows for such things as tables and chairs, mountains and streams, town clocks, people and crowds, and so on. The question of the correct characterisation of what these things have in common marking them off from nonparticulars is, however, not adequately answered by quoting this independence of existence, since without an account of such independence itself it has little meaning other than particularity, and so we are no further ahead. And anyway, how can tables and mountains be said to be independent of trees and valleys, or crowds independent of people? Perhaps the way to spell out the notion of independence is by means of other features of particulars, rather than by a direct assault.

We have had occasion to note, as an equally central feature of particulars, that they have properties – or as they are variously called also, 'attributes' or 'accidents'. Indeed the notions of particular and property go hand in hand, since a property is a property of something which is said to instantiate it. Even though not all instantiations are by particulars – the table instantiates the property of solidity, but beauty too instantiates the property of desirability – nevertheless all particulars do undoubtedly instantiate properties, even many of those properties which themselves instantiate others. It could perhaps be argued that a property's instantiating another is really no more than a particular having both those properties – beauty instantiates desirability only in that a beautiful thing is a desirable thing. Yet even if that were quite generally true, properties are had by other entities also, such as events and processes. The Second World War, for example, was an event lasting from 1939 to 1945 and so having certain temporal properties, and many other properties besides. We cannot say, therefore, that particulars simply *are* those entities which have properties, only that they do have properties just as other entities do.

Nor can we contrast particulars with events and processes by claiming that they possess their properties in a different way, particulars being notoriously able to change their properties but events and processes having a fixed set which is definitive of them. True, John Smith is many things over the years, and the event of John Smith getting married just happens when he changes one set of properties for another; but the event itself takes time, and might move from possessing interest to possessing the opposite if the vicar is slow and the participants mumble too much. And the Second World War possessed and lost many properties from start to finish. Particulars, events and processes all can therefore possess and lose properties.

Might particulars be contrasted with events and processes however in that the latter are the very exchange of properties by the former or by other events or processes? Particulars engage in such events and processes by being loci of change, by coming to possess properties and losing others. A particular can go on unchanged over a period of time – nothing happens to it – and is not therefore essentially a changing entity, but when it does change its properties then there is an event or process. But then, events and processes have the same options: they too can remain unchanged for their duration, or alternatively alter their character as they proceed. Particulars, in contrast with events and processes, do however have the peculiarity that they are not themselves changes in the properties of other things.

We have noted too, and can now admit this is another feature shared with events and processes, that particulars stand in various relations with other particulars. This is really an unsurprising implication of the fact that they have properties, since many properties are relational in character. There are two kinds of relational property which are in themselves categorial and seem, probably for that very reason, to be partially definitive of the category of particulars itself. These are, of course, the spatiotemporal properties of locations in space and time, and the causal connections between things.

1. Aristotle's subjects

An account of particulars will need to satisfy these two demands: it will need on the one hand to account for the peculiar particularity of particulars, their independent existence; it will need, on the other, to draw the contrast we have found it hard to draw between particulars and happenings such as events and processes.

An account which will satisfy these demands can be produced by suitable supplementation of Aristotle's approach to characterising primary substances. I must first note and resolve an apparent conflict in his view as expressed so far. It will help us get clear on the point that particulars are not properties, and Aristotle's central thesis that their difference (at the ontological level) reflects the contrast between reference and predication (at the level of thought and language).

The apparent conflict is that Aristotle has said that 'a substance – that which is called a substance most strictly, primarily, and most of all – is that which is neither said of a subject nor in a subject', and yet he has also identified substance as the first of the predicables. How can substances be any kind of predicable if they cannot be 'said of', that is predicated of, a subject? The way to resolve this conflict is to take the first kind of predicables to be secondary substances rather than primary substances; if we take this line, Aristotle is committed to a list of categories one larger than his list of predicables. Alternatively, we can say that Aristotle's categories consist of nine kinds of predicables and primary substances.

In the sentence 'Socrates is a man' the subject term 'Socrates' refers to the particular Socrates, and the predicate term 'a man' predicates of Socrates being a man. Now according to the general theory of predicables, being a man is being a kind of substance, so does 'Socrates is a man' involve predicating a primary substance? I do not think so. It involves predicating only a property, the property of being a man, and not predicating a primary substance as such. Socrates, the primary substance, is not predicated of anything: being a man (having that substance distinguishing property, falling under that secondary substance) is predicated of the primary substance.

For Aristotle the essential definitive feature of substances such as Socrates is that they *cannot* be predicated, 'said of' anything. 'Socrates' can never appear as a predicate term in a sentence, and in this it exhibits an exclusivity of role not shared by words for properties. A property can, like a substance, have a property predicated of it; it can, unlike a substance, be itself predicated of other things.

There are some prima facie problems with such a thesis, notwithstanding its apparent advantages. There are sentences such as 'Tully is Cicero' and 'This is John Smith' where the use of a name for a particular apparently involves a substance being said of something referred to by the subject term. This problem is solved, of course, by treating these sentences as expressing identity propositions and not as subject-predicate in form after all. There are also sentences which involve properties being said of properties, but where the subject term takes a different form from its associated form when appearing as a predicate term: 'Beauty is desirable', we say, rather than 'Beautiful is desirable', and in contrast we happily use 'white' (as a variant on 'whiteness') in either subject or predicate position. Such sentences, following John Stuart Mill,[16] can be made to conform to the Aristotelian thesis by treating the insistence on 'beauty' as a mere grammatical convention.

Aristotle's thesis has the great advantage of linking together three otherwise puzzling distinctions, and distinctions what is more drawn in different realms. The first is the distinction 'in reality' we draw between particulars and properties or 'attributes', the second the one we draw in language between subject terms and predicate terms, the third in both thought and language between referring and predicating or 'describing'. Not only that, but it suggests that the correlations between language and thought and reality are more than a happy accident. There is something in Leibniz's criticism of its being a 'nominal' explanation of the particularity of particulars, however, unless it can be supplemented with an explanation of such correlation.

The second half of Strawson's *Individuals* is devoted to precisely this question, and I can only briefly indicate his solution here. The distinction between subject and predicate is said to involve a difference in the manner in which they introduce their 'terms' (meaning by this not words but what they stand for – particulars or universals) into propositions: 'A subject-expression is one which, in a sense, presents a fact in its own right and is to that extent complete. A predicate-expression is one which in no sense presents a fact in its own right and is to that extent incomplete'.[17] Subject-expressions (at least in the case of expressions for particulars) are complete in that they involve speaker and hearer knowing 'some distinguishing empirical fact about what they introduce'. The distinction between particular and universal Strawson says involves a difference in the manner in which they 'collect their terms in assertions': 'A term may be thought of as a principle of collection of other terms. It may be said to collect just those terms such that when it is assertively tied to any one of them, the result is not only a significant, but also a true proposition'.[18] It is on the basis of the peculiar manner in which particulars collect their terms that Strawson believes he can explain the completeness of subject-expressions, why particulars are the paradigm cases for subject terms, and why particulars cannot be countenanced as predicate terms.

If we allow an explanation along Strawson's lines for the Aristotelian theory of the particularity of particulars insofar as they differ from properties, we are still owed an account of the distinction between particulars and events or processes. In fact it is only when we have got that too that we can say we have characterised our category of substance. The Aristotelian thesis needs supplementation, therefore, and this comes from another feature which we have already noted as belonging to particulars.

2. *Principles of identity*

A particular is something which has principles or criteria of identity which provides for two things, for the individuation of that particular amongst others of its kind and for the reidentification of that particular as numerically the same as on a previous occasion. Added to the Aristotelian thesis this goes a long way to uniquely describing our category of substance. Substances, our individual or particular things, are separated from each other by their criteria of identity and herein lies their special particularity or independence of existence.

To illustrate with a simple example. What is it to be a table, a *particular* table? Tables of course are items of furniture filling a certain role and a description of that role will be found in a dictionary. But being a particular table is having a unique existence distinguishable from that of all other tables. This table on which I write now is not the same as the one in the dining room. Knowing what tables are is a matter of knowing more than the dictionary definition, since it involves knowing the criteria of identity for tables. It involves, on the one hand, being able to distinguish this table and the one in the dining room and count them as two tables rather than one; it involves, on the other hand, being able to trace these tables' life histories – if not completely and actually, then at least in theory – and that requires being able to recognise a table as numerically the same as one previously encountered. Being a table is, therefore, being something which is distinguishable from others of its kind and recognisable as the numerically same thing as on a previous occasion. A particular has criteria for its individuation and reidentification, jointly its criteria of identity.

The criteria of identity for chairs will have great similarity to those for tables, and indeed so will such criteria for all those particulars which are physical objects. It is only to be expected too that these criteria will involve pretty centrally the spatiotemporal existence of physical objects. One table, for example, will be distinguished from another qualitatively exactly the same in terms of its different spatiotemporal location. And a table will be said to be the same as one previously encountered as long as there is a series of places going back in time to the time and place of the original table where each member of the series is adjacent to the next. In fact we can say that, for particulars which are physical objects, the criteria of identity come to this: the criterion for individuation is given by those features which are definitive of that kind of individual and spatially distinguish it from others of its kind; the criterion for reidentification is given by supplementation of this criterion with the spatiotemporal continuity of the object.

There are particulars other than physical objects, and we can note two quite important kinds: mental states, and the possessors of mental states, thinking things like persons and animals. Not surprisingly the criteria of identity of these two kinds of particulars make reference *inter alia* to spatiotemporal properties. Mental states, such as the particular state of believing proposition P, are datable phenomena, coming into existence and passing away. They are, moreover, the possessions of those who have them, this one being say John Smith's rather than Joe Brown's. And insofar as John Smith is a particular of a spatial kind, the criteria of identity of the state of belief will latch onto the spatial existence of ordinary physical objects. John Smith is not, of course, an ordinary physical object and we must not expect that criteria for his identity will be the same as for tables. The question of personal identity is a vexed one, persons being physical objects and at the same time possessors of mental states, and criteria of identity for persons reflect this fact.

Particulars can be of other types too, and some interesting ones are the groups formed by the types already mentioned. There are, for example, particulars such as this dining room suite, or this motor car, or indeed this chair where the particular in question can be seen as a complex of parts which may be particulars in their own right. The possibility of removing a chair from the suite, or the back seat of the motor car, and spatially distancing it from the rest of the complex provides interesting complications of the simple criteria of identity for physical objects. Once we have sorted out the question of personal identity we are faced, too, with the even more complicated questions of the identity of crowds, families, societies and so on.

We count as particulars locations, both in space and in time. Places, in other words, are treated as like physical objects in many respects, often being designated by names of their own but always being identifiable in terms of their spatial relations to other places and things. Locations in time – moments, days, years and so forth – have a similar status to places. It is not however the case that criteria of identity for places make no use of temporal facts, or vice versa for moments and so forth, since criteria for both make essential use of reference to spatiotemporal physical objects in any case and so to the other spatiotemporal dimension. Arguably too we count as particular such peculiar entities as Plato's appearance, Plato's height and so forth, properties in their instantiations by particulars of other types. Their criteria of identity inevitably make use of the criteria of identity of those instantiating particulars.

Which brings me finally to the question of the distinction between particulars and events and processes. I believe that the question is in fact wrongly put, insofar as it assumes that events and processes are not themselves particulars: it must now be admitted that this runs contrary to the parallels we have been able to discover between them. The difficulties experienced in saying how they differ from particulars are easily interpreted as reflecting the fact that they are after all particulars themselves. But as we have just now seen not all particulars are of the same kind and different particulars are identifiable in terms of their different criteria of identity. Since events involve change of properties by other particulars it must be expected that their identity depends on that of the identity of those other particulars, and since they are in themselves temporal phenomena their identity will have temporal features too. It is perhaps easiest to envisage these criteria of individuation and reidentification if we think of examples such as the Battle of Hastings or the sinking of the Titanic which are easily dated and involve previously identified particulars, and generalise from there.

Are particulars 'independent existents' in a way in which events are not? Well, events depend for their existence on the particulars which they involve, so events at least are not independent in that sense. But particulars, too, lack that sort of independence; for they, too, depend for their existence on the places they inhabit, the times they exist in and the properties they possess – at least they must have *some* spatiotemporal location and *some* properties to exist themselves. All particulars, including events, have a particularity or independent existence only in the sense explained above: they have criteria for individuation one from another, and for reidentification at different locations.

Events and processes, among particulars in general, do have some peculiarities. Aside from their involving changes in other particulars, as we have already seen, they have the special property of being introducable into propositions not just by subject terms but also by verbs: 'John Smith smiles' introduces the event by means of the verb. No other particular can be introduced like this, and a theory of events and processes could be developed along the lines of Aristotle's theory of particulars. But events and processes undoubtedly are particulars, and the proper contrast with a particular is a property or 'universal'. Many events, indeed, virtually take on the guise of physical objects, and their criteria of identity too. Hurricane Alice can move about and go through many changes, but is an event for all that.

CHAPTER 3   ESSENCE AND ACCIDENT

I. SUBSTANCE AND ACCIDENT

'Substance' is a term traditionally opposed to 'accident' or 'attribute'. Particulars are contrasted with properties, accidents or attributes which they instantiate. The metaphysical debate over the characterisation of this category has long gone under the title of 'the problem of universals'. I will look briefly at a few of the main positions philosophers have taken in a moment, but first I should point out that the characterisation of substance given in the previous chapter is by implication a characterisation of properties too. Substance and attribute, particular and property being correlative entities, what is said about the one is thereby refused of the other.

Take the Aristotelian thesis first: particulars are never said of, predicated of, anything, that is they are never introduced into a proposition by a predicate. In contrast therefore properties are predicated of other things, though they share with particulars the possibility of having other properties predicated of them. Secondly, take the fact that particulars have criteria of identity. Can properties sensibly be said to have such criteria? Can, say, the property of redness be said to have a criterion whereby it is individuated from other qualitatively identical properties, and a criterion of reidentification which allows for its recognition as numerically the same as a property previously encountered? Of course not. Properties do not have numerically distinct but qualitatively identical duplicates which a criterion of individuation could separate. If a property is qualitatively indistinguishable from redness then it *is* redness. Further, since properties cannot have criteria of in-dividuation then they cannot have criteria of reidentification either, the latter criteria being partly parasitic upon the former.

Properties therefore are contrasted with particulars in their ability to be said of other things and their lack of criteria of identity.

For Aristotle, as we saw in the last chapter, there was a kind of 'substance' which fell on the side of properties on his account – and which, we can add, shares with properties the absence of criteria of identity. Such 'substances' Aristotle called 'secondary', and for clarity's sake it would be best to note that they are not particulars at all, but a special kind of property. What Aristotle had in mind were the genera and species in which particulars participate, properties like being human, an animal, a living thing. Every primary substance, every particular, falls under a number of such classifications, and the classifications form hierarchies such that different particulars share the same species, different species the same genus and so forth. The differentiae between species can be compared to some extent to the specific differences between two particulars which make them two, but that is not to say that there are criteria of identity for species. There cannot be two qualitatively identical species which are yet numerically distinct, for that is a special mark of particulars.

Aristotle saw science as engaging in the classification of the different species of particulars, and their genera and so on up the hierarchies. He believed that nature fell into a fixed and limited set of such divisions, a set of 'natural kinds' as we would call them. With developments in science since his time we would now reject a number of aspects of this view. Darwinian evolution ensures that natural kinds are not fixed, and the physical sciences have given the lead away from a purely descriptive, classificatory science into the realm of theoretical speculation and explanation. But there are natural kinds and a description of their peculiar status among properties is a difficult one.

1. The problem of universals

The investigation of the category of properties has a long history as the problem of universals. Do properties exist at all, or is that the special privilege of particulars? A complete answer to this question must await my last chapter, which will discuss the existence of entities satisfying the fundamental features of our conceptual scheme, and I will assume for the present that their existence is at least a possibility. The theory which denies their existence is nominalism. This takes the extreme position that apart from particulars there are no other things, though of course there are all sorts of apparent assumptions of existence made in our thought and talk about reality. There are, this theory admits, general words such as 'red', 'animal' and 'justice', but their status as general words reflects rather a feature of our use of them than a feature of what they stand for. Bishop Berkeley and David Hume, to name just two, were strongly critical of the seventeenth-century version of the existence of properties, the theory of general ideas, and insisted that all ideas are particular.[1] The only thing general is our use of those ideas to stand for many things. The 'general idea' of white, for example, is no more than a particular idea variously applied.

Now an argument can be produced showing that ideas must be, in the relevant sense, general however their generality is manifested. The idea of white, for example, is intrinsically something which has application to a variety of particulars and hence satisfies that traditional and indisputable requirement on properties. Whatever the problems are of conceiving of a mental image lacking specific features, as Locke's theory of general ideas seems to suppose, the generality of ideas or of properties cannot really be disputed. But that is what nominalism does, in effect. Only language is general in its application, the theory says, and there are no entities as such which have instantiation in various particulars. The general term 'white' applies to a whole host of things which we call white, but not because these things share the property of whiteness. The only thing they share is their having the term 'white' applied to them.

Unattractive as this view is, it must be admitted that it grows out of dissatisfaction with alternative accounts which do have their own problems. Plato took properties to have a very exalted kind of existence, to be in fact the most real things in the universe: in contrast, particulars inhabited a shadowy, unreal world of appearance.[2] Properties were treated as ideals of which particulars were poor 'copies', 'imitated' in an imperfect manner, in his analogy to explain the possession of properties by particulars. This theory of Forms – the usual translation of Plato's term *Eidē* – was designed to serve many philosophical functions other than this one and is admirable in that it does so quite neatly. It does not represent an acceptable solution to the problem of the possession of properties, however.

Plato's theory says that, for example, circular things are circular because they partake of, imitate or share in the Form of Circularity. The Form is an entity which exists in a special non-spatiotemporal realm of Forms, and is the Ideal or Standard of Circularity. It is itself circular *par excellence* and all other things are a poor shadow of Circularity Itself. The objections are plain. Circularity Itself, that which is shared by all circular things, cannot sensibly be said to be circular – any more than the Form of Smallness can be said to be small, or the Form of Duration to endure. Worse, and Plato was acutely aware of this problem,[3] the theory is trying to explain possession by many things of a common property by introducing something else which possesses that property too. His own way of putting his reservations about this was to say that it leads to an infinite regress. Partaking of the Form, imitating it, 'sharing in it' apparently require some third thing (the 'third man') for the circular particulars and the Form of Circularity to 'share in' to explain *their* similarities. And so on.

Plato's difficulties here were seen by Aristotle as a direct consequence of treating properties as themselves particulars, and standing in relation to properties in just the same way as particulars do.[4] His own resolution of the difficulties was to place properties wholly and squarely in the world of particulars themselves, taking their existence to be totally dependent on that of particulars. There is no such thing as Circularity Itself, only particular things which are circular. The property is found in the particulars which instantiate it, and not somewhere else. A kind, like the human species, is not some separate entity which exists or can exist quite independently of human beings but exists in and through the particulars which instantiate it. This is not nominalism, however, since it does not deny the existence of properties altogether: it rather provides an account of their existence, and added to the thesis that particulars are not said of anything else, quite a good one.

Perhaps as a consequence of developments away from a

picture of the fixed species and genera in nature many philosophers have come to deny that properties as such exist as well as the resemblances between particulars, and in the spirit of nominalism have seen our property terms as the conventional erection of certain resemblances into properties. This resemblance theory faces the objection which Russell among others has put: are not resemblances themselves general, not just particular, and hence does not this form of nominalism commit itself to at least one kind of universal?[5]

2. *Essential accidents*

I have contrasted 'substance' with 'attribute' or 'accident', and those latter two terms certainly have been used interchangeably since the seventeenth century. Before then, a tradition going back to Aristotle would have drawn a contrast between essential and accidental properties or attributes, and therefore between essence and accident. Locke's rejection of the scholastic doctrine of substantial forms which stood squarely in the Aristotelian tradition allowed him to use 'attribute' and 'accident' interchangeably: other philosophers have followed the same practice.

But now essentialism is once more back in fashion, and we seem stuck with the infelicitous expression 'essential accident'. The distinction is once more drawn between those properties which are possessed *essentially* or *of necessity* and those which are possessed *accidentally* or *contingently*. With this contrast in mind it makes perfect sense to refer to 'essential accidents' and 'accidental accidents'. Properties which are possessed of necessity by a particular, another property or a kind are said to exemplify '*de re* necessity' as opposed to '*de dicto* necessity'.

This last contrast can be drawn as follows, allowing for the sake of argument that numbers have some or even all of their mathematical properties essentially. The sentence 'The number of the planets is 9' ascribes a purely contingent, accidental property to the number 9 but that of course is not a mathematical property of the number. The sentence '9 is the result of adding 4 to 5' ascribes a necessary property to the number 9, an essential property the possession of which is part of what 9 *is*. But contrast with this 'Bachelors are unmarried'. This too appears to ascribe a necessary property to its subject, so does it not correspond to the sentence '9 is the result of adding 4 to 5'? The difference, according to the tradition being described, is that the former sentence ascribes a necessary property only in the sense that what the sentence expresses is necessarily true *as a matter of linguistic usage*, since bachelors are unmarried by definition; the latter sentence ascribes a necessary property in the quite different sense that what it expresses is necessarily true *as a matter of fact about the number 9*. The former sentence is an example of *de dicto* necessity, the latter of *de re* necessity. *De re* necessity is what characterises the relationship between essential, nonaccidental, necessary properties (essential accidents) and their possessors.

The assumption that numbers have essential properties is not one I want to seriously maintain, since it is arguable that the relationship between numbers has the same status as that between bachelors and being married, that is that it is a matter of *de dicto* necessity only. Numbers do however seem to be the best illustration of the *de re* modality thesis, since it is very plausible to claim that there are no *de re* properties at all. We saw in Chapter 2 that Kripke, among others, has recently argued for the thesis that particulars have essential properties which they possess in all possible worlds, and we saw the problems with that thesis. A particular seems to have only contingent properties, except in that it has necessarily whatever properties are part and parcel of the kinds which it instantiates: of course Socrates being human involves him necessarily being a living thing, but there is no *de re* necessity about Socrates being human.

Aristotle thought that species had essential properties; that, for example, the species man had as such a property 'being rational'. The function of science was to classify species according to these *de re* necessary properties, 'seeing' their necessity after gathering many cases by an act of intellectual intuition.[6] The idea of *de re* necessity as applied to kinds is illustrated too by such claims as Descartes' that the essence of mind is thought, of body extension, and Leibniz's that the essence of the human mind is its knowledge of eternal necessary truths. (Leibniz[7] actually produced an argument for God's existence from the fact that there are essences, since these essences must exist somewhere and where else could that be but in God's understanding?) And these philosophers would take mathematical truths such as plane triangularity involving having angles equivalent to two right angles as illustrative of *de re* necessity too.

The mathematical examples can be treated like the arithmetical ones – they arguably illustrate *de dicto* necessity only. What of the properties of other kinds? There seems to be no good reason for taking the properties of kinds as anything other than contingently possessed by them, except in trivially necessary cases such as being human involving being an animal which are obviously cases of necessity *de dicto*. What properties together form a kind *naturally*, that is in nature and not as a consequence of definition, seems to be a contingent matter. Hydrogen and oxygen do in fact combine and it is even contingent that the natural consequences of that combination are those properties, chemical and physical, which are the properties of water. How then can being made from hydrogen and oxygen be in any sense a *necessary* feature of water, how can the natural kind water be said to have this property as a matter of *de re* necessity? The same seems to be true of natural kinds quite generally, and since there are no other candidates for the *de re* necessary possession of properties we should conclude that no such things exist.

The Aristotelian tradition has been revived, however, by philosophers such as Kripke and Putnam,[8] and *de re* modalities are once more favoured in an account of our thought and talk about natural kinds. Natural kind terms are said to be another example of rigid designators. I will look first at Locke's account of natural kind terms, before assessing this contemporary version of the thesis that natural kinds have essential properties.

II. NATURAL KINDS

A recent book by J. L. Mackie gives a reasonably clear minimal interpretation of what philosophers have meant to pick out by the term 'natural kind': the phenomenon is the lawlike clustering of properties. I call this interpretation minimal since it makes no commitments concerning either the use of natural kind terms or the existence of *de re* essential properties of such phenomena. Mackie gives, as examples of natural kinds, 'chemical elements and compounds (as opposed to mixtures) such as gold, water, and common salt, and the various species of plants and animals'. He goes on:

> There are natural kinds because properties are not randomly and independently distributed among things, but tend to cluster. We can say *roughly* that wherever we find some set of properties – those that could be used as a defining set for, say, cats – we also find many other properties common to the class of objects picked out by the first set, including a number of other sets of properties each of which would serve as an alternative defining set for that class, being distinctive of, as well as common to, cats.[9]

(He adds that this is rough because not all cats have the properties that are in general typical of cats.)

I will improve on Mackie's characterisation only by adding some more examples of *non*-natural kinds, that is kinds of things which we have words for but which do not pass the 'clustering of properties' test. Apart from Mackie's chemical mixtures (soil would be one example) there are artefacts such as chairs, boats and shoes; and there are kinds within the species human picked out by their social roles – such as presidents and kings. These are only examples of this class of kinds which are not thought to fall under the heading of 'natural': the general idea is that certain kinds seem to be marked off for us by nature itself, nature having bestowed on them a mass of properties which await our discovery and which give sense to the idea of a *correct* classification of substances and species.

Both the Lockean and Kripkean accounts of our use of natural kind terms can be introduced through the distinction which Locke makes between the nominal and real essences of substances. Natural kinds are examples of what Locke calls substances, which he contrasts with modes and relations. He writes of 'ideas of substances' as

> . . . such combinations of simple ideas as are taken to represent distinct particular things subsisting by themselves,

in which the supposed or confused idea of substance, such as it is, is always the first and chief. Thus if to substance be joined the simple idea of a certain dull whitish colour, with certain degrees of weight, hardness, ductibility, and fusibility, we have the idea of lead; and a combination of the ideas of a certain sort of figure, with the powers of motion, thought, and reasoning, joined to substance, make the ordinary idea of a man.[10]

In contrast, modes and relations do not subsist by themselves: modes, for instance, are 'such complex ideas which, however compounded, contain not in them the supposition of subsisting by themselves, but are considered as dependences on, or affections of, substances' and he gives as examples the ideas signified by the words 'triangle', 'gratitude' and 'murder'. The basic thought is one I have supported in Chapter 2, that individual substances are what subsist by themselves.

We divide our ideas of substances into those of individuals such as this rabbit, this man, this lump of gold, and those of substance kinds such as rabbit, man and gold – Aristotle's primary and secondary substances. Now Locke distinguishes, for substance kinds, and in particular for natural kinds, between the nominal essence and the real essence.[11] The nominal essence of a kind is the complex abstract idea (the complex of ideas) which we take to stand for various properties of the kind in terms of which we recognise it to be what it is, in terms of which we assign particular things to that kind. The nominal essence of gold, for example, is the idea of a yellow, shining colour, great weight in proportion to size, malleability, fusibility and so forth. The nominal essence of man would be the idea of a certain sort of figure, with the powers of motion, thought and reasoning.

But, thinks Locke, there is something else about a kind which warrants the term 'essence' just as much, namely the real internal constitution of the kind which is responsible for its having those features, ideas of which figure in the nominal essence. This second sort of essence he calls the 'real' essence, and if we drop the reference to ideas in drawing the distinction it can be put like this: the *real* essence of a kind is the actual internal constitution of the substance, a constitution shared by all particulars of the same kind; and this gives rise to those properties with which we are acquainted by observation, and by which we recognise these particulars as of that kind, the *nominal* essence. So, for example, the internal real essence of gold will be the special atomic structure which distinguishes gold from other elements, and the nominal essence will consist of the consequent observable properties, powers and capacities by which we recognise a piece of metal as a piece of gold.

1. Locke's linguistic nominalism

I will, in passing, put aside two quite interesting aspects of Locke's discussion as not of great import for my present theme. One is his antagonism towards the scholastic version of natural kind theory, the theory of substantial forms.[12] Locke's fundamental objection to that theory was to its assumption that substance kinds could be recognised a priori, and that an a priori scientific classification of substances could be achieved which was more than an unfolding of definitions which we ourselves have given to terms. In pressing this insistence on the futility of such 'progress', Locke is led to make the nominalist claim that kinds are all of our own making, so regrettably denying the existence of natural kinds. The other issue, which I have already discussed in Chapter 2, is Locke's view of the idea of substance in general. This 'something, we know not what' which underlies those properties that distinguish one substance kind from another is, as we saw in the above quotations, an element in individual ideas of substances also, but a pretty vague or obscure idea.

Accepting that there are natural kinds, and that such things as gold have an internal real essence and an observable nominal essence, the question arises as to how natural kind terms are used. It would seem that we must use terms such as 'gold', 'rabbit', and 'water' to signify the relevant kinds in such a way that some properties of the kinds are integral to that signification: how else could such terms find a reference? Things must be taken to be gold, water or rabbits in virtue of some features which make gold, water and rabbits what they are. Now the question is: what features of natural kinds are thus integral to the use of natural kind terms? Would the correct answer be that such terms pick out those kinds in virtue of their observational properties, which figure in what Locke calls the nominal essence; or do they pick them out in virtue of their internal 'hidden' constitutions, their peculiar real essences?

'Between the nominal essence and the name there is so near a connexion', Locke writes, 'that the name of any sort of things cannot be attributed to any particular being but what has this essence, whereby it answers that abstract idea whereof that name is the sign.'[13] The nominal essence of gold is integral to the use of the term 'gold': we can say, even more forcibly, that the observational features of gold constitute the content of the idea of gold, that they are the attributes connoted by the term 'gold'. But Locke complicates the picture by noting how men – 'especially such as have been bred up in the learning taught in this part of the world' – put something more into their use of substance terms, namely a reference to the internal real essence as well. 'Men do suppose certain specific essences of substances, which each individual in its several kinds is made conformable to and partakes of, . . . and thus they ordinarily apply the specific names they rank particular substances under to things as distinguished by such specific real essences.'[14] And he is clearly not thinking only of the scholastic tradition, but referring to real essences here in his sense of the internal constitution from which the properties of the nominal essences flow.

Having noted this common practice of men to go beyond the nominal essence in their use of natural kind terms, Locke points out the futility, as he sees it, of such a practice. If we knew the real essences of kinds it would make sense to base our classification on them in terms of such properties, but Locke thinks we do not (did not and would not) have such knowledge. We are presented with the features making up the nominal essences of the substances of the world, and it is clearly the thing to do to associate those known features with our substance terms. Putting it another way, it is pointless to attempt to classify kinds in terms of features other than those with which we are acquainted.

Locke's 'linguistic nominalism' as we may call it is clearly indefensible, and that for at least two reasons. In the first place it is dependent upon a clear distinction being drawn between those properties which are observable and those which are not, a distinction which is at the very least blurred by the continuous developments in science with its sophistications of observation techniques, new instruments and revisions of definitions of preexisting descriptive terms. To illustrate the last point, take for example the way in which a term such as 'magnetic' has changed with greater knowledge of even the everyday observable properties of magnetic materials, how for example developments in electromagnetism have changed the meaning of the term which earlier was associated simply with the behaviour of lodestones. And the change in 'observational meaning' of the term reflects associations drawn by science between previously unassociated or even unknown phenomena – the production of electricity when a magnet is moved in a coil, for example. The simple division between observation and theory, for long a central tenet of empiricism, is certainly not beyond question.

Yet even if we did not question that, it is certainly not the case that science has remained as ignorant of the deeper 'hidden' non-observational properties of matter as Locke assumed it would. Locke's account of the use of natural kind terms is based on this pessimism which, while not unfounded in his day, has been greatly replaced by what we now regard as substantial knowledge of such properties. Science has developed in leaps and bounds, not just in the study of physical materials but in biology also. These sciences all classify their objects of study on the basis in part of the newly revealed deeper mechanisms of nature, a great many of the so-called observational properties of matter having been traced to the properties of the microscopic parts of different materials. There is therefore no argument on the basis of ignorance to sustain the Lockean distinction between real and nominal essences, and the consequent linguistic nominalism which associates natural kind terms with nominal essences.

It is worth pointing out, before going on to Kripke's alternative account of our use of natural kind terms, that Locke's account at least does not involve the error of taking kinds to have criteria of identity. Both real and nominal essences of the different materials and species in nature are but the properties specific to those kinds, the correct assumption being that – even though some more properties may be discovered which those kinds have – there are no kind duplicates which share these nominal or real essences. Nominal and real essences both belong peculiarly to the kind in question, and in that sense only are 'criteria of identity'; they do not provide for the individuation of one kind from another which is qualitatively indistinguishable.

Moreover, Locke's account does not commit him to a belief in essential properties, *de re* necessary properties of the natural kinds, notwithstanding his multiple use of the term 'essence'. Nominal and real essence are both simply the properties which the kind has, with no sense being thereby given to the notion of what properties the kind has *necessarily* as opposed to *accidentally*. It is left to Kripke to introduce such *de re* necessities into an account of natural kinds. Kripke does this, what is more, in a way which uses these necessary properties as the foundation of criteria of identity across possible worlds.

2. Kripke's linguistic realism

Locke, then, associates natural kind terms with nominal essence. If some parcel of material has all the relevant observable properties, powers, dispositions and so on, then that parcel of material is gold; the internal constitution does not come into the question. Kripke, on the contrary, associates the term with the real essence of the substance, so that if this parcel of material has the proper internal structure it is gold and the observable properties do not come into the question. Kripke does not treat the real essence of a substance as part of the meaning of the substance term, but takes this essence as nevertheless integral to the use of the term. 'Gold', 'rabbit' and 'water' are ascribed to parcels of matter in virtue of those parcels having the relevant internal constitution. Natural kind terms do not have meaning, do not connote these properties, but rigidly designate the kind – hence they refer to the same kind in all possible worlds, where sameness of kind means sameness of real essence.[15]

Before seeing how Kripke develops this idea let us briefly ponder a couple of claims made by Mackie in favour of a Kripkean use of natural kind terms.[16] Mackie's first suggestion is that a Kripkean use is peculiarly suited to explanatory science, insofar as explanation in science frequently or usually takes the form of revealing the internal constitution of substances which give rise to observable features of the world. Yet this feature of scientific explanation should not be taken to establish that the Kripkean account is a true account of our use of these terms. It is clearly true that the real essence of substances could not figure in the use of substance terms in the absence of explanatory science, simply because they would not in that event be known. It is also true that the scientist typically takes the real essence of substances into account in his classification of materials – think, for example, of the classification of elements on the periodic table. It does not by any means follow that explanatory science depends on some prior Kripkean use of natural kind terms, or that some *complexes* of real and nominal essence properties are not associated with these terms. Indeed Mackie mentions terms like 'sleep' and 'jaundice' which illustrate the fact that a phenomenon can be identified purely in terms of its observational features and yet be provided with a scientific explanation. (Even better examples would be sensory phenomena such as sweetness.) Explanations in terms of the internal structure of substances would not be ruled out by a Lockean use of natural kind terms, so the existence of explanatory science hardly shows the Kripkean account to be the correct one.

The second point Mackie makes, if I understand him correctly, is that a Kripkean use of these terms is the guarantee that people are not talking at cross purposes, associating such words with an idiosyncratic collection of observation terms. In fact Mackie represents himself here as simply following Locke's explanation of our unfortunate tendency to relate natural kind terms to what he saw as the unknowable real essences of things, namely that this ensures that we are all talking about the same things when they use these terms. The problem arises of course from the fact that natural kinds are not marked off by nature by means of a limited range of properties in the case of each kind, but rather by a host of properties connected together. Each person will have some limited range of such properties in mind when he uses the natural kind term – the nominal essence by which *he* recognises, say, a piece of gold as gold – and there is no guarantee that from person to person the range of properties will not vary. Indeed, there is every reason to expect that these ranges will vary to some degree, depending on each person's experience of the kind in question. How, then, do they succeed in communicating?

Locke's solution, if Mackie's interpretation is right, is that each man secretly refers his term to the hidden constitution of the substance, and as this does not vary from person to person the same thing is being talked about. It is, I think, difficult to see this as any solution at all. For one thing, people (all people, according to Locke, and most people in fact) have no conception of what this internal constitution is, so the meaning of the natural kind term cannot be altered by making such a reference. For another, the real essence secretly referred to by any user of a term like 'gold' is presumably identified as that responsible for the limited range of properties making up the nominal essence of gold for that speaker, and the properties of yellowness and malleability (to give one possible example) are presumably the outcome of parts of the real essence of gold different from those parts which are responsible for some alternative nominal essence such as fusibility and great weight for size.

Locke thought in fact that our use of natural kind terms was always going to be found wanting. There is no way that our knowledge even of the observable properties, powers and capacities of gold or water could ever be complete, so we could never associate our terms with an exhaustive nominal essence and in that way guarantee identity of reference from speaker to speaker. Mackie is right of course in his suggestion (made against the background of much-improved scientific knowledge) that a Kripkean use of terms would overcome the problem: but this does not in itself recommend a Kripkean use to us. For there is one simple expedient whereby the problem can be overcome, identity of reference secured for all speakers, though terms be applied in a Lockean manner in association purely with nominal essence: this is of course that speakers agree on the nominal essences of natural kinds, agree on the group of properties, powers and capacities which they will all take as connoted by the term. That is certainly within their capacity as speakers of the language, for it is done (as Locke himself admits) for modes and relations such as 'murder' and 'triangularity', and it is done standardly in law to make precise legal judgements; there is no apparent reason why the same could not be done for 'rabbit', 'water' and 'gold'.

The claim that natural kind terms are rigid designators is, however, not offered as a recommendation for the use of our natural kind terms but as a thesis about the way those terms are actually used, and must be assessed in that spirit. In brief, the thesis is that a natural kind term, being a rigid designator, operates as a referring device with no descriptive content; it designates the *same* kind in all possible worlds; and sameness of kind is sameness of real essence. The consequence of this thesis is that natural kinds have essential, *de re* necessary properties, which are those of their real essences.

To take an example.[17] Water is a natural kind, and our term for it designates that kind without connoting properties like being liquid, being tasteless, being colourless, or consisting of hydrogen and oxygen. The term 'water' is a referring term, not a descriptive one. However, we discover that water is made out of hydrogen and oxygen, so our term 'water' *does* designate the substance H_2O, this being the real essence. It follows that the term 'water' designates H_2O in *any* possible world, not just the actual world, no matter what other properties we imagine water to have or lack in such possible worlds. If there is a substance in a possible world which has *all* the phenomenal properties our water has in the actual world, but is made out of hydrogen and chlorine, it would not be designated by our term 'water'; if a substance with the real essence H_2O is present but having very different phenomenal properties from those exhibited by our water, even being poisonous, acidic to the taste, solid to very high temperatures, and so on, it *would* be the substance designated by 'water'. Kripke would say the former substance would not *be* water, the latter would be.

I think the Kripkean thesis allows for even more bizarre cases than this, the idea behind it being that there are possible worlds where substance kinds share with those of the actual world their real or nominal essences, but possess very different essences of the other sort. Just how bizarre this can be is shown by the fact that any such breakdown in our actual world's real-nominal essence connections represents a breakdown in the natural laws governing the real world. Could water have the appearance of a rabbit, or rabbits be made simply of

chlorine?[18] I can see no way of restricting the idea of possible
worlds to exclude these cases on Kripke's approach. Requiring
that all possible worlds share with the actual world its laws of
nature is tantamount to denying there can be worlds which
have substance kinds sharing one or other of the real-nominal
essence divide. And then natural kind terms could not be said
to be rigid designators, since the point of that claim would be
lost. That point is to insist that we can distinguish between the
de re necessary properties and the contingent properties of the
kinds. Water has the essential property of being made of H_2O,
but also contingent properties such as liquidity at normal
temperatures.

Part of this picture, too, is that kinds can have, in possible
worlds, all the phenomenal characteristics of kinds in the actual
world; so there can be kinds that are qualitatively
indistinguishable, contrary to my insistence that properties in
general (of which kinds are a special case) do not have
numerically distinct but qualitatively identical doubles. The *de
re* essential properties are the means whereby the identity of
kinds is secured, which provide in other words criteria of
individuation and reidentification across possible worlds. Not
only is Kripke treating natural kind terms as equivalent in
function to proper names, he is also treating kinds as a sort of
particular. We should remember Aristotle's diagnosis of the
problems of Plato's theory of Forms.

The assumption that our use of natural kind terms
presupposes the kind of split between real and nominal essence
that this picture involves is highly implausible. The function of
science is precisely to discover the natural laws linking the more
recherché properties of matter with the various powers,
capacities and tendencies exhibited by natural kinds, links
which are usually thought of as cases of 'natural necessity'
though contingent and empirical. Of course these necessities
have nothing to do with the *de re* necessities of Kripke: that
water is essentially H_2O and so has that constitution of
necessity is quite different from the 'necessity' as science sees it
of the consequent phenomenal properties. Yet the implication
of this activity of science is that our natural kind terms are used
in a way which does not allow for, does not countenance as a
possibility, the kind of real-nominal essence split Kripke

envisages after those discoveries have been made. Before, yes: but that is a matter simply of 'epistemic modalities', as Kripke has explained the term, simply a matter of 'for all we know, things might be so-and-so'. We *know* that water is H_2O, and that this is liquid at normal temperatures, tasteless, essential for life and so on, and the connection between these things. All this is part of our use of the term 'water', and we would be at a total loss what to say about a 'possible world' in which these properties split apart. Our use of 'water' relates to *this* world, and has nothing to do with imaginary examples.

'Water could be solid, acidic to taste, poisonous' we say, and do not mean this to express our ignorance. Yet all it expresses is the contingency of the grouping of properties to form a kind. And 'Water could be HCl' equally appears quite acceptable as expressing the same kind of contingency. There are no *de re* essential properties of natural kinds.

I must repeat, too, the criticism made of Locke's theory in the last section, that it assumed too simple a division between theoretical and observational properties. That criticism is equally valid against Kripke's approach. What is more, the reservations expressed in Chapter 2 about possible worlds in connection with names as rigid designators are obviously as relevant here. Possible worlds are far from being philosophically transparent entities, and hold no promise of philosophical clarity. But then, they are not relevant to an account of our actual practice with natural kinds and their terms in any case.

A point deserving a brief mention is that Kripke's *de re* modalities might seem, on closer scrutiny, to be really a form of *de dicto* modality in the final analysis. The theory is put forward, not so much as an account of what natural kinds are like but directly as an account of the way our practice of referring to natural kinds presupposes them to be. In that case it is a thesis about language, not reality. This is wrong, though, in that it assumes again the kind of opposition between reality and our thought and talk about it which makes categorial description seem of little consequence. Kripke's thesis is, undoubtedly, a thesis about language use, but so was Aristotle's thesis that particulars cannot be predicated.

One issue on which I think Kripke is right is his insistence on the lack of contradiction in the description of some truths as 'necessary but *a posteriori*', as for instance in the example that 'Socrates is a man' or 'Water is H_2O'. (This is not, by the way, to say that these truths *are* necessary but a posteriori.) Others have insisted on the point that the notions of necessary truth, a priori truth and analytic truth are such as to leave open the possibility of a sentence expressing a necessary truth which is at the same time neither analytic nor a priori. Harré and Madden, for example, in their book *Causal Powers*[19] do this.

One way in which Kripke's empirical necessities differ from Harré and Madden's ought nevertheless to be stressed. They take themselves to be expounding a theory of causation which is very Lockean, and indeed rests on the distinction between nominal and real essence. Briefly (since this is considered in Chapter 4 below), they take as the central notion in their account that of a 'powerful particular': particulars (e.g. pieces of matter, members of species) have various observational properties of a dispositional kind, where these properties flow from the internal constitution of these particulars. Necessity, in their view, characterises the relationship between the internal constitution and these dispositional properties – or, more simply, between real and nominal essence. The scientist tries to discover what are the laws of causal necessitation at work in nature and what he discovers are therefore empirical necessities.

We can understand, I believe, something if not all of the way Harré and Madden are using the expression 'necessity' here in terms of the demands of scientific explanation: an explanation, it might be said, should show why such and such things *must* be so; why, for example, fire *must* consume wood, water *must* be liquid at usual room temperatures, and so forth. Locke too thought a knowledge of real essence would show why the various substances *must* have the features included in their nominal essences. Necessity, then, is coming in at least in the context of explanation; the necessities discovered by the scientist are precisely those which provide the explanations for which he seeks. Kripke's necessities, on the other hand, seem to be totally independent of any explanatory role, for his theory is precisely separating real from nominal essences. How could the necessity, for example, of water being H_2O – that is, there being no possible world in which water is not H_2O – be connected in an explanatory way with the nominal essence properties of water in our world which might be lacking in other worlds?

CHAPTER 4   CAUSATION

I. TWO PROBLEMS: CAUSE AND THE CAUSAL PRINCIPLE

The physical world is composed of particulars, both physical objects and animated objects. These particulars stand in spatial and temporal relations one to another, which relations are for the most part constantly changing. Particulars are, what is more, frequently related to one another in an interactive way, in that they causally affect one another. A primary problem for any metaphysical enterprise which engages in categorial description is to understand this relation.

The two obvious questions are what, precisely, does this relation comprise, and what are the precise terms of the relation? These two questions are not totally independent, though it is not always clear just how answers to one of them limits the range of possible answers to the other.

Another problem concerns the reign of law in the world of particulars. This again involves two subordinate questions: is nature uniform, i.e. do like causes always produce like effects; and does everything that happens have a cause? This last question is indeed at the heart of the perennial problem of the freedom of the will. If everything is caused, how can people exercise a freedom of choice in their actions?

In recent philosophy the 'problem of causation', which involves all these matters, had led to questions concerning the analysis of those peculiar properties which are dispositional, and to that of the analysis of conditional statements. Such statements include what are called 'contrary-to-fact' conditionals such as 'If kangaroos had no tails they would topple over' for which it has again been thought necessary to reintroduce Aristotelian essentialism.

I will not be able, in this present chapter, to do justice to all aspects of the problem of causation, and since the category of causation is our primary object of investigation I will say little about the problem of the reign of law. That, in any case, has figured as an assumption in the kind of traditional metaphysical speculation which went beyond categorial description, and is clearly associated with that other principle of the intelligibility of the universe, the principle of sufficient reason. My discussion will concern the category of causation itself and the difficult problem of how to construe contrary-to-fact conditionals.

1. Aristotle's four causes

Before entering into these contemporary issues concerning our category of cause I must briefly expound Aristotle's doctrine of the 'four causes' in order to show that we need not recognise a similar number of kinds of causal entity in our categorial account. As Ackrill has recently pointed out, the Aristotelian doctrine might better be called 'a doctrine of four "becauses"': Aristotle is distinguishing different sorts of answers that can be given to the question "Why?" or "Because of what?" '.[1] The usual appellation suggests Aristotle was committed to four kinds of causal phenomena, perhaps one genus with four species. A succinct if enigmatic exposition of the doctrine is given by Aristotle himself as follows:

> A thing is called a cause in one way if it is a constituent from which something comes to be (for example, bronze of the statue, silver of the goblet, and their genera); in another way if it is the form and pattern, that is, the formula of its essence, and the genera of this (for example, 2:1, and in general number, of the octave), and the parts present in the account; again, if it is the source of the first principle of change or rest (for example, the man who deliberates is a cause, and the father of the child, and in general the maker of what is being made and the changer of what is changing); again, if it is as a goal – that is, that for the sake of which (for example, health of walking – Why is he walking? – we say: 'In order to be healthy', and in so saying we think we have stated the cause).[2]

The four things distinguished here as 'causes' are four factors which might figure in explanations concerning some particular phenomenon. Following Aristotle's own examples, the 'material cause' explanation is exemplified in an appeal to the matter of the goblet to explain its tarnishing; the 'formal cause' or 'essential cause' explanation in an appeal to the mathematical relationship between notes in acoustic theory; the 'efficient cause' explanation in appealing to the father as producer of the child; and the 'final cause' explanation in an appeal to the desire for health in explaining why someone is walking.

Clearly, accepting Aristotle's formal and material 'causes' does not require us to recognise causal *entities* comparable to efficient causes; we are required to countenance only formal and material cause *explanations*. What such explanations refer to are substances and their essences, and we have already sufficiently made room in our categorial description of our thought and talk for these. We are therefore not called upon to expand our list of categories in this direction.

Final causes are a different matter. The very failure to sufficiently emphasise the peculiarity of final cause explanations, and the special kind of entities appealed to in such explanations, has led to much confusion. If final cause and efficient causes are taken as the same kind of thing we get the puzzle of how causation can possibly happen *backwards* – how later health can possibly be the cause of earlier activity – as well as the question of how something can be caused by a later state which fails, for fortuitous reasons, to materialise. In the case of human action the usual solution is to invoke the *intention* to achieve some goal, a state or event preceding the action, as the cause of the action and in that way to save the correct temporal order of causal operation. But this solution is not so readily available for all examples of final cause explanation, and in any case is not needed but for the conflation of final and efficient causes. What we really need to do is to recognise the special status of explanation in terms of goals, reasons, purposes and intentions, and more generally in terms of the functions served by actions and events in animate and inanimate nature.

But do we need therefore to recognise a special category of final causes, on a par with the category of efficient causes?

Actually, we need to recognise that goals, reasons, purposes, intentions, and so on are all distinct sorts of things which are better not conflated under the one notion of final cause. It is, in fact, better to keep the idea of 'final cause' closely wedded to the idea of explanation, rather than forging a special category of being under that name. In any case, all these different sorts of things figuring in final cause explanations are overshadowed, both historically in metaphysics and in terms of fundamentality in our thought and talk about reality, by efficient causes. It is the notion of an efficient cause which is categorial.

II. DOES CAUSATION INVOLVE A NECESSARY CONNECTION?

1. *Locke versus Hume*

Of those issues which have divided philosophers in their search for an account of our category of cause, central since the seventeenth century has been whether such an account need introduce a 'real connection' between a cause and its effect. The opposing views can justifiably be called Lockean and Humean, for John Locke took causes to *necessitate* their effects and so to have a real tie with those effects which goes beyond spatial and temporal proximity, whereas David Hume saw causation as nothing more than the uniformity of coexistence of cause and effect in spatial and temporal proximity. We will look at the way in which these opposing views have been developed, and how they are represented in the work of contemporary philosophers.

Locke's position, from which we can usefully begin, involves a necessary connection between a cause and its consequence, that is the belief that consequences *must* follow from their causes. Fire has a power to melt gold, for example, so that placing a piece of gold in a fire results in its melting: but this consequence does not just happen to follow, it *cannot but* follow. Gold must melt when fire is applied to it.

The origin of our concept of power, and our ideas of the individual powers which belong to particular substances (such as gold and fire), Locke takes to be our experience of change in our environment. 'The mind being every day informed by the senses of the alteration of these simple ideas [qualities] it observes in things without ... considers in one thing the possibility of having any of its simple ideas changed, and in another the possibility of making that change; and so comes by that idea which we call *power*. Thus we say fire has a power to melt gold'.[3] Moreover, we acquire the clearest idea of power from the action of our will on our minds and our bodies: 'We find in ourselves a power to begin or forbear, continue or end several actions of our minds and motions of our bodies, barely by a thought or preference of the mind. . . . This power . . . is that which we call the will'. Power and cause are two notions very closely associated. Locke writes: 'Power being the source from whence all action proceeds, the substances wherein these powers are, when they exert this power into act, are called *causes*; and the substances which thereupon are produced, or the simple ideas [qualities] which are introduced into any subject by the exerting of that power, are called *effects*'. The fire, which has the power to melt gold, is therefore designated the cause, and the melting of the gold is the effect.

Finally, Locke holds that the effect of any cause is necessitated by it in a very strong sense. If we knew the real constitution of fire, for example, we would see that gold placed in it *must* melt, '. . . as all properties of a triangle depend on and, as far as they are discoverable, are deducible from the complex idea of three lines including a space'. If we knew the real essence (or, as we would now say, the microstructure) of any substance, we could deduce its effects; we could *see* what consequences it must have on other things, as well as what colour and so on it must itself have.

The analysis of causation was a central issue in Hume's philosophy of nature, and a good deal of his thought is directly aimed against the kind of view held by Locke. Basically Hume seeks to give an account of nature which is well adapted to our experience of it, and he insists that we have no experience of power or necessary connection as such. Our experience of causation is simply one of objects which are constantly conjoined; as far as the observation of causation is concerned, it comprises the contiguity in space and time of what we call the cause and the effect, the precedence of the cause on the effect, and (most importantly) the constancy of the coexistence of things like the cause with things like the effect. 'We say, for instance, that the vibration of this string is the cause of this particular sound. But what do we mean by that affirmation? . . . That this vibration is followed by this sound, and that all similar vibrations have been followed by similar sounds.'[4] Beyond this, we have experience of no other connections between causes and effects.

Locke would cheerfully have accepted that our experience was limited in this way. 'Were the power or energy of any cause discoverable by the mind, we could foresee the effect, even without experience, and might, at first, pronounce with certainty concerning it by the mere dint of thought and reasoning', writes Hume,[5] and Locke would agree with him that we are never in fact able to infer effects simply from their causes. Yet, according to Locke, we can arrive at the idea of power or necessary connection by *inference* from our experience, this being the real import of his account as described above. Such a claim is unfortunately incompatible with the basic empiricism of both Locke and Hume: 'No reasoning can ever give us a new, original, simple idea, as this philosopher himself confesses' Hume writes. Locke ought to have held that we have no such idea, unless it had been derived directly from experience or compounded out of such ideas.

Locke thought our experience of our wills provided direct experience of power, an idea Hume finds easy to demolish. In the *Inquiry* he devotes (perhaps unnecessarily) five pages to its refutation, and discusses it in an appendix to the earlier *Treatise* where he writes: 'So far from perceiving the connexion betwixt an act of volition, and a motion of the body, 'tis allow'd that no effect is more inexplicable from the powers and essence of thought and matter. Nor is the empire of the will over our mind more intelligible. The effect is there distinguishable and separable from the cause, and could not be foreseen without the experience of their constant conjunction'.[6] We do not experience a power or necessary connection, but must discover from experience just what influence our will has on our minds and bodies, '. . . and experience only teaches us how one event constantly follows another, without instructing us in the secret connection which binds them together and renders them inseparable'.[7]

The connection between a cause and its effect cannot, Hume concludes, contain a necessity such as Locke postulated. Causation can be nothing more than contiguity, succession and constant conjunction. 'All events seem entirely loose and separate. One event follows another, but we never can observe any tie between them. They seem *conjoined*, but never *connected*.' Hume offers this as his formal definition of a 'cause': 'An object followed by another, and where all the objects, similar to the first, are followed by objects similar to the second'; or as he writes in the *Treatise*: 'An object precedent and contiguous to another, and where all the objects resembling the former are plac'd in like relations of precedency and contiguity to those objects, that resemble the latter'.[8]

To understand the development of Humean theories of causation it is useful to introduce the technical notions of 'necessary condition' and 'sufficient condition'. In the context of our discussion we can understand these notions in the following way. Let 'C' stand for an object, event or quality of one kind, and 'E' for one of some second kind. Now, to say 'C is a sufficient condition of E' is to say 'C's are always accompanied by E's', in other words 'Whenever C exists then E exists also'. A simple example is that the application of a stretching force to a piece of steel raises its temperature, so that we can say that stretching is a sufficient condition for the steel becoming warmer. And to say 'C is a necessary condition of E' is to say 'E's are always accompanied by C's' or 'E never exists without C'. Interestingly enough, the same example can serve here: the steel's becoming warmer is a necessary condition of its being stretched. (It should be clear from the example that where C is a sufficient condition for E, E is a necessary condition for C.) For another example we can use Hume's case of the vibrating string which produced a particular tone: here the vibration of the string is always accompanied by the emission of the tone, so we can call the vibration a sufficient condition of the tone which itself is therefore a necessary condition of the vibration. A further example would be that the presence of oxygen is a necessary condition for life and life therefore a sufficient condition for the presence of oxygen.

It is plain that Humean theorists of causation can find these two technical terms very useful in expressing their views, for they are claiming that causation is a matter of some form of repeated sequences of those phenomena which we call cause and effect, with no further element of necessitation. How, precisely, must we represent Hume's account in these terms? There is unfortunately some ambiguity in his talk of causation as constant conjunction, for this might be construed as saying that C's being the cause of E's means (i) that C is a necessary *and* sufficient condition of E or (ii) that C is a sufficient condition of E. If C and E are constantly conjoined (as, for example, a particular vibration of air and a particular tone) then we never have one of them without the other; but if C is always conjoined with E, it might be possible to have E in the absence of C (as the vibration of this particular string is always joined with a particular tone, but so are the vibrations of other *similar* strings).

If Hume is saying (i) his definition is open to the objection that effects can be brought about by more than one cause: death, for instance, can be the result of poison, disease, old age, and so forth; evaporation of water can be brought about by raising the temperature or lowering the air pressure. It would not be plausible to argue that a different effect is produced by these different causes, so C's being the cause of E cannot be a matter of C being a necessary and sufficient condition of E. In fact, a close perusal of Hume's words in his explicit definition in the *Inquiry* and *Treatise* makes alternative (ii) a more plausible interpretation of his intention: for Hume, C's being the cause of E is nothing other than C being a *sufficient* condition of E.

When we look carefully at Hume's theory it must strike us that he has given little indication of the terms which are related by causation, of what causes and effects are in themselves. It is a disturbing feature of Hume's writings that he pitches them at a very theoretical level and stops to give examples only rarely. In his definitions he talks of causes and effects as 'objects', both in the *Treatise* and the *Inquiry*, but this is a vague term. One example of causation given in the *Treatise* is that 'motion in one body is regarded upon impulse as the cause of motion in another', and here causes and effect seem both to be processes or qualities rather than objects in any straightforward sense. Another example is that 'the motions of our body, and the thoughts and sentiments of the mind . . . obey the will', where perhaps 'objects' in some extended sense would serve to describe cause and effect since here particular existents are being referred to. The examples in the *Inquiry*, notwithstanding the official definition in terms of 'objects', seem to suggest that causes and effects are events, or perhaps properties of particulars: the impulse of one billiard ball is attended with motion in the second; an act of volition produces motion in our limbs; the vibration of a string is the cause of a particular sound.

An objection to Hume's definition which goes more to the heart of his intentions is this: not all sufficient conditions are in fact causes, and not all causes are in fact sufficient conditions. Examples are easy to find to illustrate both cases. Night is invariably followed by day, and so is a sufficient condition of it according to the meaning assigned to that technical term above, but we do not regard night as the cause of day. A clock striking 6 o'clock in a Manchester factory is followed invariably by people leaving factories in other cities, but the clock's striking is hardly the cause of those events. These examples show that sufficient conditions do not always constitute cause–effect relationships. Though obviously we would want to insist in both examples that there is an underlying causal process or set of causal processes which would explain these sequences, there is no reason to think that the same must always be true – a rainfall in some part of England may indeed always be followed by fishermen in Japan drinking tea, but that is not the cause of their doing so. And in any case Hume theory is still undermined.

Examples showing that causes need not be sufficient conditions include the following: plucking a string may be the cause of a particular sound, but not if the string is in a vacuum in which case the plucking would not be followed by the sound; striking matches may well be the cause of their lighting but not when the matches are damp or the surface too smooth. Causation, therefore, would not be manifested by uniform sequences of events and hence cannot be equivalent to sufficient conditions. What is more, a possibility which cannot be ruled out a priori given contemporary science is that there is a fundamental indeterminacy in nature so that some event might cause a second in one case but not in a precisely similar case.

Quite apart from these problems, a strong case can be made out for saying that Hume fails to sustain the sufficient condition analysis, and ultimately is committed to acknowledging a necessary connection after all. This can be argued on two grounds. In the first place, part of the aim of his writings is to indicate the origin of the very idea of a necessary connection which is involved in our conception of causation. In the second place, one of his own definitions of cause, which we have yet to see, involves that very notion.

First, then, our idea of causation does involve on Hume's account something more than spatiotemporal contiguity, succession and uniform coexistence – it does, after all, involve a necessary connection between the cause and the effect. 'An object may be contiguous and prior to another, without being considered as its cause. There is a *necessary connexion* to be taken into consideration' he admits. The problem, as he sees it, is to explain how such an idea arises, for our experience of causation seems simply to be one that is adequately described without it. Hume considers one of his greatest philosophical achievements to be the discovery of its origin. As far as the experience of an individual cause–effect sequence is concerned, no basis for the idea can be found; but 'after frequent repetition, I find, that upon the appearance of one of the objects, the mind is *determined* by custom to consider its usual attendant, and to consider it in a stronger light upon account of its relation to the first object. 'Tis this impression, or *determination*, which affords me the idea of necessity.'[9] After frequent experience of things of type C followed by things of type E, the very experience of a new example of C leads us, by what Hume calls 'a felt determination of the mind', to expect an example of E. This provides the origin of our idea of necessary connection, but at the same time Hume believes he has shown the illegitimacy of applying the idea to causal sequences themselves. 'Upon the whole, necessity is something, that exists in the mind, not in objects; nor is it possible for us ever to form the most distant idea of it, consider'd as a quality in bodies. Either we have no idea of necessity, or necessity is nothing but that determination of the thought to pass from causes to effects and from effects to causes, according to their experienced union'.[10]

This is basically confused. Insofar as Hume has provided an

adequate account of the origin of our idea of necessary connection, he has after all vindicated Locke's claim that our idea of causation does involve it. What is more he can hardly insist that the idea, once attained, is illegitimately ascribed to something simply because it is not from that thing that we have attained it – that would be to espouse an empiricism stricter even than Locke's. The idea, once arrived at, ought to be attributable to a wider range of phenomena than that, and why not to the cause-effect sequences in the world? The greatest difficulty in Hume's position is that it requires him to sustain a distinction between what our conceptual scheme takes to exist in the world and what actually does exists there, for he has admitted that our *idea* of causation involves a necessary connection even though no such thing exists in the world. This raises large issues which I discuss elsewhere in this book, but suffice it to say that a simpler and more palatable distinction could have been adopted at this juncture by Hume, namely that between what our conceptual scheme takes to exist and what we *directly experience*. Though our experience is of uniformities adequately described in the terminology of necessary and sufficient conditions (if it indeed is like that), why should we limit outselves to a world without Lockean necessities?

As for the second ground for accusing Hume of lapsing into a Lockean account, this is Hume's unfortunate definition in the *Inquiry*, where after giving his sufficient condition account he writes: '. . . or, in other words, where, if the first object had not been, the second never had existed'.[11] Far from being another formulation of the sufficient condition analysis, this looks like a necessary condition one. Fire, it says, is the cause of the gold's melting because the gold would not melt without it, and that means that fire is a necessary condition of the melting. But worse than that, it goes beyond even a necessary condition analysis, for it takes us into the realm of contrary-to-fact suppositions, and a necessary condition analysis would concern only what *does* happen in the way of uniformities. Suppose, it suggests, that contrary to fact the fire had not been applied to the gold: then the gold would not have melted. Now if fire is a necessary condition (in our technical sense) of gold's melting, this says nothing about what would happen in such hypothetical situations, for it is logically consistent with this that the gold would have melted anyway: necessary conditions concern only what *does* happen and not what would or might happen, or would or might have happened. The step beyond actual uniformities to contrary-to-fact hypothetical situations is a very great step towards a Lockean theory, for how could it be thought that the gold *would not* have melted in the hypothetical situation unless in the actual case of a fire-melting sequence the melting is necessitated by the fire and not just a conjoint but disconnected phenomenon?

2. *Mill and Mackie: modern Humeans*

Hume's account is clearly unsatisfactory, and seems to lead back to Locke's starting point. Before looking more closely at Lockean theories I will, however, trace some of the developments of Hume's theory in the work of John Stuart Mill in the nineteenth century and of the contemporary philosopher J. L. Mackie.

Mill's *System of Logic* (first published in 1843) essentially tries to establish a system of rules for the discovery and proof of scientific laws, the most important of which are for Mill the 'laws of sequence' or cause and effect. He provides a careful discussion of causation which, nevertheless, leaves many issues obscure. Like Hume he sees causes as sufficient conditions of their effects, and to some degree improves on Hume's specification of the terms of the relation. 'For every event', Mill writes, 'there exists some combination of objects or events, some given concurrence of circumstances, positive and negative, the occurrence of which is always followed by that phenomenon'.[12] An event is very rarely (if ever) a consequence of a single antecedent but follows from a complex of antecedents '. . . the concurrence of all of them being requisite to produce, that is, to be certain of being followed by, the consequent'. Though every one of the antecedents is necessary for the consequent – and is, therefore, within the context in which the consequent occurs, a necessary condition of that consequent – Mill is very clearly aware that we normally designate just one such antecedent as 'the cause' and refer to the others merely as 'conditions'. 'Thus, if a person eats of a particular dish, and dies in consequence, that is, would not have died if he had not eaten of it, people would be apt to say that eating of that dish was the cause of his death. There need not, however, be an invariable connection between eating of the dish and death: but there certainly is, among the circumstances which took place, some combination or other in which death is invariably consequent', and he goes on to indicate that the total conditions would include a particular bodily constitution and a particular state of health.

Mill's analysis is undoubtedly more subtle and sophisticated than Hume's, with this recognition of the complexity of causes, the status of individual conditions as necessary in the circumstances for the consequent, and a recognition of our common practice in selecting some among them to designate as 'cause'. 'The cause, then, philosophically speaking', he nevertheless insists, 'is the sum total of the conditions positive and negative taken together; the whole of the contingencies of every description, which being realised, the consequent invariably follows'. In these pages Mill provides an illuminating discussion of the ways in which we make our (philosophically unjustified) selection of 'the causes'. He would have found acceptable such suggestions as Collingwood's[13] that we select as the cause of an event 'the handle, so to speak, by which we can manipulate it. . . . The cause of a bruise is the kick which a man received on his ankle; the cause of malaria is the bite of a mosquito . . .'; and that of H. L. A. Hart and A. M. Honoré[14] that 'the notion, that a cause is essentially something which interferes with or intervenes in the course of events which would normally take place, is central to the commonsense concept'; acceptable, that is, as long as they are not erected into an analysis of causation which makes it anything other than the sufficient condition of the effect. And Mill's account is subtler than Hume's in making very clear provision for the plurality of such sufficient conditions, the 'plurality of causes'.

Mill improves on Hume too in the clarity of his specification of the causal terms. Effects being for him always events, causes are or include events, processes, the continuing properties of things or even 'negative conditions' which are the *absence* of any of these things. Undoubtedly all such things can be designated 'cause' in common parlance, even though they each present a question to be addressed by the metaphysician rather than any final answer to the analysis of causation. One sophistication over Hume's theory is nevertheless also something of an embarrassment for Mill, namely, his recognition of counteracting causes. Suppose a cause of E comprises the set of positive conditions C1, C2, C3 and the set of negative conditions −C4, −C5. Mill recognises that a cause can be prevented or counteracted by another (as striking a match will not cause it to light if the match has been dampened) and tries to adapt his account to this. Counteracting causes would, on his theory, be positive conditions such as C4 and C5, which figured as negative conditions in the cause of E. That this is a failure on Mill's part is obvious from the fact that such conditions could only be causes in a sense other than the official definition for they are not sufficient conditions themselves. What is more, the sufficient condition analysis is clearly now under threat, for that requires that causes are essentially a matter of *what always happens*. How can causes fail, then, to produce their effects?

Perhaps Mill can be defended on this matter in as much as he never actually limits his notion of 'cause' to positive conditions alone, always including the negative ones as well. There is nevertheless one point at which the theory does clearly break down, interestingly in a way very similar to Hume's downfall. Mill realises that, after all, it is not enough to say that causes are sufficient conditions, for there are sufficient conditions which are not causes. Night follows day but is not caused by it, as we have already noted. He writes: 'If there be any meaning which confessedly belongs to the term necessity, it is *unconditionalness*. That which is necessary, that which *must* be, means that which will be whatever supposition we make in regard to all other things. The succession of day and night evidently is not necessary in this sense'. And he concludes: 'Invariable sequence, therefore, is not synonymous with causation, unless the sequence, besides being invariable, is unconditional'.[15] Now Mill is here obviously trying to save his sufficient condition account by treating *unconditional* invariance as nevertheless a special form of invariance, with necessity seen as nothing more than invariable sequence in the end. Mill is obviously also unsuccessful, as these quotations show. Unconditionalness is to be understood in terms of contrary-to-fact conditionals, for it implies that an event C which is the cause of E would still have brought about E *even if other things had been different.* If eating a balanced diet is the cause of a good complexion, not only does it always produce a good complexion it will do so 'whatever supposition we may make in regard to all other things'. Why, we may ask, should that be so unless there is a necessary connection between the cause and the effect? Indeed, if we may change Mill's words into the terminology of possible worlds, unconditional invariance is invariance in (a specially circumscribed subset of) all possible worlds, which we will later see has been thought a plausible interpretation of Lockean necessity.

Mill's failure to maintain the spirit of his uniformity analysis had its parallel in Hume, for they both found it necessary to take the step beyond mere uniformities to contrary-to-fact conditionals. The same is true of the last of the Humeans I will look at, the contemporary philosopher J. L. Mackie, for whom this step is moreover combined with a further fault which we found in Hume's account.

In a paper called 'Causes and Conditions', Mackie presents an analysis of the statement 'A caused B' which is heavily dependent on Mill's work yet departs from it in interesting ways. What we usually mean by an assertion of the form 'A caused B' is, according to this analysis, not that A was a sufficient condition, a necessary condition or even a necessary and sufficient condition of B. What we mean is something more complicated: '. . . the so-called cause is . . . an *insufficient* but *necessary* part of a condition which is itself *unnecessary* but *sufficient* for the result'.[16] For obvious reasons Mackie abbreviates this to 'an INUS condition', and illustrates it with the simple example of a short-circuit being the cause of a fire. The short-circuit is an INUS condition because, in combination with other factors (some of which, in Mill-like fashion, would have been negative factors), it led to the fire, though clearly by itself it was incapable of doing so and there are other ways in which the fire could have started. Interestingly, this analysis has the implication that causal statements do not specify what other conditions contributed to the effect, they only presuppose that there were such other conditions.

This INUS condition account forms the basis of Mackie's treatment of causation in this paper, and is offered again in his complex and sophisticated work *The Cement of the Universe*.[17] A major innovation in that book is however the introduction of a non-Humean account of our causal language, of the *concept* of causation with which we operate in contrast to an account of causality as it exists in the objects in the world. Mackie now sees the INUS condition analysis as providing an accurate reconstruction of our causal statement only if it introduces something more than complex regularities. A's being an INUS condition of B is interpreted in a counterfactual sense – so that B *would not* have come about in the circumstances, if A *had not* occurred. 'Necessary' and 'sufficient' conditions are here being given senses other than our technical ones, and the INUS condition analysis has become more Lockean that Humean in its import. Mackie's account of the contrary-to-fact implications of causal statements is of much intrinsic value, and Lockeans can clearly learn from it, but it does represent the quite typical breakdown of Humean analyses. And it leaves Mackie with precisely the problem facing Hume himself, that the theory offers one account of our concept of causation and a different, purely uniformity, account of causation in the objects of the world themselves; and this division between our concepts and what they are about is very difficult to sustain.

3. A modern Lockean theory

We have seen that Humeans are quickly led to introduce some element into their account which is alien to their uniformity intentions, so we must look more closely at the Lockean alternative. I have given much space to Hume and his allies because the onus of proof must be on his approach, the greater part of the philosophical world being persuaded that causation involves a real connection of necessitation – whatever that comes to. Some, indeed, including Kant whose theory of nature places the problem of causation in a central philosophical role, have taken this very fact to show that the concept of cause cannot have been derived from experience. Such philosophers would roundly reject the empiricism of Hume.

We will look therefore at a contemporary attempt to develop a Lockean necessity theory, but first let us ask whether Locke succeeded better than his rivals in his specification of the causal terms. Causes, for Locke, are substances: but what precisely did he intend these to be? The choice lies between *kinds* of stuff (such as gold and fire) and particular instances or samples of such kinds (pieces of gold, individual fires), which we called 'particulars' – in other words, between Aristotle's secondary and primary substances. The argument for saying Locke intended kinds is that we seek to explain phenomena in terms of those microscopic properties of matter which are common to all particulars of a kind, and such seems to be what Locke means by the real essence of substances. On the other hand, he does talk of the power and hence the causal efficacy of the will, and do not wills vary in their causal efficacy? Assuming we opt for kinds rather than particulars as the true Lockean view, we still face the question whether he means substances as identified in respect of their real or their nominal essences. As we saw in Chapter 3, he is insistent that the terms of science are terms designating substances in respect of their nominal essences – by water, we do not refer (as we would say) to H_2O, but to a colourless, tasteless liquid having such and such other properties – and so we should perhaps opt for the latter interpretation, and yet he clearly wants to locate the origin of the causation in the primary qualities of substances which constitute their real essences.

Effects are, for Locke, either substances themselves or the qualities of substances. Interestingly they are not events, although it would here matter little if we loosely interpreted Locke as seeing effects as the creation or destruction of substances, or the alteration of their qualities. One kind of causation which Locke's terminology lends itself to quite well is that whereby the microstructure of salt, for example, is causally responsible for its *own* peculiar taste and appearance as well as for its improving the taste of food or dissolving in water. It does seem clear enough that, in the case of effects, substances are effects in respect of their nominal essences and the qualities which are effects are observable qualities, for the powers which Locke refers to are powers to produce observable changes. Here Locke is most closely wedded to his own empiricism.

A strong challenge to the Humean regularity view has recently been developed by R. Harré and E. H. Madden.[18] Owing much to the ideas of Locke, particularly his distinction between the real and nominal essences of substances, this theory is worked out in some detail and is claimed to have the virtue of fitting well both with actual scientific practice and the commonsense account of experience.

The central notion of Harré and Madden's theory is that of the 'powerful particular', and it is, according to them, about such particulars that we occupy ourselves in our ordinary dealings with the world and in science. 'When we think of causality and action', they write, 'we look to such images as a springtime plant forcing its way upwards towards the light, as the pulsing, surging movement of the protoplasm within the amoeba.'[19] This contrasts strongly with the examples typical of the thinking of the Humeans, such as the moving billiard ball which strikes another so effecting motion in it. Now particulars are seen to have certain causal powers and abilities, that is, they have dispositions which are exhibited in various circumstances, and these are to be explained by reference to the nature or real essence of those particulars. A piece of copper, for example, will expand when heated and will conduct electricity when a potential difference is applied to it, and a glass of sulphuric acid will burn the skin and turn litmus paper red: such dispositional properties are their powers and abilities, to be explained in terms of the real constitutions of the particulars acting and acted upon. Finally, the theory locates the necessity which the authors believe characterises causality in the relation between (i) the nature of the particular and the occasion for the exercise of one of its powers (or abilities), and (ii) the manifestation of that power (or ability). More briefly, natural necessity relates natures and powers: something with *that* nature *must* exhibit *this* reaction in relevant circumstances, as something with copper's constitution *must* conduct electricity.

We could say that, for Harré and Madden, causation is primarily a relation between the nature and a dispositional power of a particular, whereby its nature necessitates or causes the power; derivatively, causation is a relation between the nature of the particular and the event which manifests the power, whereby the particular in a given environment necessitates or causes the event in virtue of its nature. In both cases there is a major departure from most contemporary Humeans who treat causation as relating events, such that some one event is the cause of a contemporaneous or later event. In this Harré and Madden would claim an advantage for

their Lockean theory from the fact that science clearly does seek
to explain events by looking into the hidden mechanism of the
world, by investigating the real essence of particulars.
Moreover, the scientist is typically involved with seeking the
causes, not of this or that individual event but of *types* of events,
for he wants to know why copper conducts electricity and why
sulphuric acid is caustic, and he looks therefore to the real
essences of things.

The evidence is not, however, all on the side of the Lockeans.
We are not always looking for an explanation of types of events,
even though our explanations must serve as a pattern for other
cases, for we frequently want to know such things as why the
brakes failed or why Vesuvius erupted in 1978. Here we are
content to discover some event such as the severing of a pipe or
rapid increase of gaseous pressure which is responsible for these
results. Typically, as well, in ordinary life such cases remain
close to the surface of things and do not directly involve the real
essences of the materials concerned. Science does however have
this further commitment, yet even here it is plain that causation
is most frequently taken to link event with event, even though
the link is itself a consequence of the real essences of things. We
speak normally of the application of heat to copper (an event)
which causes it to expand, rather than the real nature of copper
as causing the expansion when heat is applied. The language of
science, perhaps, has been influenced more by Hume than by
Locke.

Probably the greatest advantage Harré and Madden claim
for a necessity account of causation is that it eliminates the
curious problem of induction which the work of Hume made so
important. One of the 'central pillars of the Humean theory'[20]
is Hume's claim that there is no contradiction in principle
between the assertion that an event has happened and the
denial that its consequence followed, and Harré and Madden
believe their theory disproves this simply by showing just
where the contradiction lies. The problem of induction, the
problem of saying why the future should be expected to be like
the past, they take to be a consequence of Hume's claim: that
claim implies a contingent connection between natures and
powers so that a change in the course of nature could be
explained neither by reference to causal powers nor by

reference to changes in the natures of particulars themselves. Hume's problem does not go away, however, with the adoption of a Lockean necessity theory. The problem of induction is as much a problem about our knowledge of the world as the world itself, and a necessity theory does not make knowledge easier to acquire. Even admitting necessary causal connections it is an a posteriori contingent matter which of them exist, and an open question whether we have correctly identified them. This can be seen as a consequence of the fact that necessity, though it goes beyond universality or regularity, nevertheless includes it. Harré and Madden do not deny that connection, yet they insist that causal necessity is something which can be observed. If necessity implies regularity, though, how can the observation of just a single case provide causal knowledge? They really have not made out a case for a Lockean approach on the basis of Hume's problem of induction.

Connected with this failure there is, nevertheless, an important contribution from Harré and Madden. We have seen that Locke and Hume both associated a knowledge of the real constitution of matter with an ability to predict a priori what effects it must have. How, it must have seemed to them, could C necessitate E unless something in C made it possible to foresee E as the inevitable consequence? Harré and Madden, on the contrary, take the nature–power connection to be necessary but a posteriori, something to be discovered by experimentation. Our explanatory practice in science does seem to fit this better than Locke's account for we do not expect our theories of the microscopic nature of matter to *entail* the phenomena which they are invoked to explain: we explain the melting of solids in terms of a particular kind of molecular rearrangement, yet such a rearrangement could as easily have resulted in quite the opposite effect. Harré and Madden have the advantage over Locke here, yet the real danger arises now that they have no role remaining for their necessary connection to play. If they remove in this way the archaic and unfortunate suggestion of an a priori science which Locke had incorporated into his philosophy, they leave the necessity in causation as an unexplained and isolated element of our metaphysics. Some attempt must be made to remedy this state of affairs, if such a notion is to be given any clear content, at the very least by relating the necessity of causation to contrary-to-fact conditionals along the lines suggested by Mackie.

III. CAUSATION AND THE CONTRARY-TO-FACT CONDITIONAL

1. *Counterfactuals: the problem*

I have already indicated the way that an account of causation inevitably leads, with the failure of an out-and-out Humean regularity account, to the problem of contrary-to-fact conditionals. On Hume's own very unrepresentative third definition, to claim C as the cause of E is to say that if C had not happened (contrary to the facts) then E would not have happened either. A causal powers approach to causation has the same connection working between powerful particulars and what would happen if circumstances were other than they are. Dispositional properties, and such there undoubtedly are in nature, themselves demand the introduction of contrary-to-fact hypotheticals: to say, for example, of a piece of glass that it is brittle is to say (at least in part) that if it were being struck hard at the moment it would break. And, of course, any attempt to spell out what necessity in nature could be will take reference to such counterfactuals as an essential part of the story.

The simplest, and hence intuitively the most attractive, approach to understanding counterfactual is that recently adopted, among other authors, by J. L. Mackie.[21] The counterfactual 'If kangaroos had no tails they would topple over' is really an abbreviated form of an argument, beginning with the contrary-to-fact supposition 'Kangaroos have no tails' and arguing on the basis of other assumptions about relevant laws of nature to the conclusion 'Kangaroos topple over'. Counterfactuals are valid or invalid, rather than true or false, and the concept of causation is shown to have a covert reference to the intentional activities of supposing and arguing. Mackie's own inclination, as already noted, is to drive a wedge between this concept of causation and a second, regularity concept and take the latter as what really matches reality. I will attempt to show the fundamental difficulty in that move in my last chapter, and will note here only that Mackie's account of counterfactuals can stand without it.

Mackie's theory is not without its problems, of course, but these do not seem insuperable. The major one is the need for the theory to spell out what constitute the 'relevant laws of nature' which, together with the antecedent of the counterfactual, will entail the consequent. In particular, the theory must give a plausible story about the way we go about our selection of these laws, and this will involve reference to the common assumptions of the speakers and hearers who are proposing and considering the counterfactual in question – the 'relevant laws' presupposed are presumably not just (or perhaps not even) the true laws of nature, but ones which are assumed to be true by the parties to the conversation. Secondly, the theory must provide room for the peculiar fact that we are able to accept contrary counterfactuals: not only do we countenance the hypothetical 'If kangaroos had no tails, they would topple over' but we can at the same time accept 'If kangaroos had no tails, they would *not* topple over', since we presume Mother Nature would have provided some other solution to the problem of balance. Thirdly, since many antecedents in counterfactuals will already run foul of at least one true law of nature, 'relevant laws of nature' which we consider along with the antecedents must explicitly exclude some which we consider to be true. We do countenance, for example, hypotheticals which begin 'If copper did not conduct electricity . . .', 'If ideal gases did not obey Charles' law . . .' and so on, and were these antecedents combined with all laws we believe to be true we could infer literally to any conclusions whatsoever: from a contradiction anything follows, according to classical two-valued logic.

None of these problems seem insuperable for Mackie's theory, and neither do others which have been raised by his critics. For example, it is easy to adapt the theory to accord with the fact that antecedents of counterfactuals typically do not entail their consequents simply with the addition of assumed laws of nature, but require certain assumed facts of a non-general kind as well – gravity is assumed to persist in the hypotheticals concerning kangaroos. And the theory as it stands will at best handle counterfactuals which are not embedded within more complex sentential construction, such as appearing as themselves the antecedents of more complex hypothetical sentences. On the face of it, these problems can all be found natural solutions, and if so Mackie's theory can be accepted as a plausible account of the contrary-to-fact implications of our causal thinking. In particular, we will not need to assume that this part of our thought and talk about reality involves us in a belief in the existence of possible worlds.

2. *A modern analysis by Lewis*

Lewis's book *Counterfactuals*[22] represents an extension of recent work in the semantics of intentional logic, an approach which construes the necessity operators in terms of possible worlds. Lewis's concern is with the if-then sentential connective that appears specifically in counterfactual conditionals, and he introduces it against the background of the (now standard) possible-world semantics for modal terms in general. Accordingly, strict conditionals are defined as material conditionals preceded by some necessity operator (e.g. $\Box(f\rightarrow g)$) and counterfactuals are exhibited as both like and unlike these. The technicalities may be intrinsically interesting, yet any philosophical interest lies in the explanatory power of such an approach in relation to our thought and talk about causal relations between things in the world, and concerning this there are grounds for pessimism. Possible-world semantics has a way of unifying a whole array of linguistic forms but many will find that in itself a 'success' of doubtful value. Those who are not averse to such a technical approach in philosophy may nevertheless question the pivot on which this particular theory turns, for possible worlds are not philosophically transparent entities.

To take a simple case, the counterfactual 'If kangaroos had no tails, they would topple over' is said to be true on the condition that kangaroos lacking tails *do* topple over *in those possible worlds which are closest to our world*. More generally, the analysis proceeds as follows. Our world is just one (the *actual* one) of the multitude of *possible* worlds and bears a varying degree of overall similarity to each of the rest. The non-actual worlds can be imagined to be arranged in a system of concentric spheres, with the actual world at the centre, in such a way that each sphere progressively further from the centre contains

worlds which are overall less similar to our world than those in the sphere before. A counterfactual – a sentence of the form 'If it were the case that f, then it would be the case that g', which Lewis writes as 'f $\square\!\!\rightarrow$ g' – is true of (or at) our world on the condition that the closest antecedent worlds (in the smallest antecedent permitting sphere) are all worlds in which the consequent holds. More fully yet, the analysis is this:
f $\square\!\!\rightarrow$ g is true at a world i (according to the system of spheres S)
      if and only if either
(1) no f world belongs to any sphere s in S, or
(2) some sphere s in S does contain at least one f world, and f $\rightarrow$ g holds at every world in s.[23]

Lewis's possible world approach to counterfactuals is in a number of ways comparable to a theory developed by Stalnaker,[24] though it has the advantage over the latter in not assuming the existence of a *closest* possible world. The major rival to this approach is the theory (or family of theories) which Lewis calls 'metalinguistic', represented by the account offered by Mackie which we looked at briefly above: on the metalinguistic approach the hypothetical f $\square\!\!\rightarrow$ g is true (or in Mackie's version valid) if suitable premisses are available which together with f allow the derivation of g.

Lewis takes this rival seriously, even to the extent that he tries to eliminate the rivalry by deriving a version of it from his own analysis. This is I think one of the weak points in the book, not just in tending to obscure the differences between the approaches but also in the perverse construal it involves of the notion of 'cotenability'.[25] On the metalinguistic account the 'suitable premisses' must be cotenable with f, i.e. would not be ruled out by the truth of f; on Lewis's definition, however, h is cotenable with f at i only if some f world is closer to i than any -h world. It is, of course, an effective misconstrual.

As for the differences, these can be seen firstly from the fact that, from the point of view of a metalinguistic theorist, Lewis would introduce irrelevant considerations in assessing a counterfactual. Lewis requires that some f.g worlds bear greater *overall* similarity to our world than any f.-g world if f $\square\!\!\rightarrow$ g is true and this demands that *all* features of these worlds are considered; in contrast, taking for example a counterfactual supported by laws, the rival account demands consideration only of those features of our world specifically relating to possible connections between the characteristics mentioned in f and g. Secondly, the rival theories can assign different truth-values to at least some counterfactuals. Worlds which depart from our natural laws with the odd small miracle might be more similar to ours than some which stick rigidly to the laws but inevitably differ on many particular facts, and on such grounds Lewis's theory would allow miracles to disrupt precisely those ties between antecedent and consequent characteristics that the rival theory would take as establishing a counterfactual connection.

The second most fundamental notion in the account (after that of possible worlds) is that of comparative similarity, about which Lewis is interesting and persuasive. The notion may well be accused of vagueness, yet it is vague in 'a well-understood way'. Moreover, counterfactuals are also undeniably vague in their truth conditions. 'Overall similarity consists of innumerable similarities and differences in innumerable respects of comparison, balanced against each other according to the relative importances we attach to those respects of comparison', he writes. One arrangement of spheres around a world i represents but one overall assessment of similarity, in terms of which $f \,\square\!\!\rightarrow g$ can be judged true; another permissible arrangement might make $f \,\square\!\!\rightarrow g$ at i false – but this is as it should be. Not all arrangements are permissible, indeed, but no one is mandatory. Such is Lewis's treatment of the 'semantic indeterminacy' or 'pragmatic ambiguity' of counterfactuals as it has been variously called.

Two consequences of Lewis's analysis deserve specific comment. In the case where f is impossible, $f \,\square\!\!\rightarrow g$ is vacuously true for any g.[26] This is an unfortunate consequence since an account of counterfactuals should discriminate (as we do) between what is and what is not counterfactually implied by impossible antecedents. 'If the contents of this jar were a body of ideal gas, it would obey Boyle's Law' is one we might favour even though it could not be, just as there can be no frictionless planes nor perfectly elastic bodies. The other salient consequence is that $f \,\square\!\!\rightarrow g$ is true if f and g are both true,[27] a point with which the metalinguistic rival will rightly take issue. Perhaps both of these consequences could be eliminated by fairly simple modification of the theory, so it would be unfair to reject it on these grounds alone.

Moving on to the central and most fundamental notion, that of possible worlds, Lewis has this to say:

> I emphatically do not identify possible worlds in any way with respectable linguistic entities; I take them to be respectable entities in their own right. When I profess realism about possible worlds, I mean to be taken literally. Possible worlds are what they are, and not some other thing. If asked what sort of thing they are, I cannot give the kind of reply my questioner probably expects; that is, a proposal to reduce possible worlds to something else. I can only ask him to admit that he knows what sort of thing our actual world is, and then explain that other worlds are more things of *that* sort, differing not in kind but only in what goes on at them. Our actual world is only one world among others. We call it alone actual not because it differs in kind from all the rest but because it is the world we inhabit.[28]

Lewis is here taking a strong realist line on possible worlds, going beyond what we have seen to be the stance of Kripke. Most philosophers might find a possible-world analysis of counterfactuals acceptable as an interim account, with a reductive analysis to follow – in terms, perhaps, of sets of sentences or (as Mackie suggested) in terms of supposing and arguing. Lewis is uncompromising: more than just a primitive notion of his analysis, possible worlds are irreducible, 'respectable entities in their own right'. Metaphysically suspect as they are for the standard reasons of obscurity or parsimony, Lewis makes a brave defence of his realism claiming that it is forgivable in being only quantitatively and not qualitatively unparsimonious. 'You believe in our actual world already;' he writes; I ask you to believe in more things of that kind, not in things of some new kind'.[29]

But one problem facing such a view is the question of the inhabitants of such other worlds – are they identical with those of this world? Lewis suggests that individuals (if not universals) inhabit only one world, but have counterparts in others, which suggestion seems again open to the charge of lack of parsimony.

Moreover, if we did allow for possible worlds how could we deny *im*possible worlds existence too? Lewis writes:

> I believe that there are possible worlds other than the one we happen to inhabit. If an argument is wanted, it is this. It is uncontroversially true that things might have been otherwise than they are. I believe, and so do you, that things could have been different in countless ways. But what does that mean? Ordinary language permits the paraphrase: there are many ways things could have been besides the way they actually are. . . . Taking the paraphrase at its face value, I therefore believe in the existence of entities that might be called 'ways things could have been'. I prefer to call them 'possible worlds'.[30]

Yet I believe, and so do you, that there are many ways in which things could *not* have been; that for example it could not be the case that there are on this desk two pencils and less than two pencils, that given the present laws of nature and other relevant conditions kangaroos could manage to stand up if they had not got tails, and so on. We seem to have the same reason to believe in *im*possible worlds as possible worlds, and the claimed parsimony of the possible worlds hypothesis is again threatened.

However, the real problem with possible worlds is that they are not needed in giving an account of the way in which we handle counterfactual claims and hence in describing the causal category. The advantages which come from their introduction stem only from their aforementioned ability to unify an otherwise motley array of linguistic forms exhibited by the possible-world semantics of intentional logic. In other words, in the absence of a sufficient refutation of the rival account of counterfactuals in terms of supposing (and this *is* an activity whose existence is undeniable) there is no reason from the point of view of categorial description for recognising the existence of possible worlds. Possible worlds function as a useful unifying device in intentional logic, not as a feature of our actual causal thought and talk. And really there are no impossible worlds even though there are ways in which things could not have been. The way to understand what this means is, it seems, to make reference to the act of supposing.

CHAPTER 5   SPACE AND TIME

I. PARTICULARS AND SPATIOTEMPORALITY

My account of particulars, or 'primary substances' as Aristotle called them, was given in two parts. The first was that particulars differ from properties in that they cannot be predicated of anything but always occur in the subject position in propositions. This was taken from Aristotle's own writings, but did not account for the peculiar *particularity* or independent existence of particulars, and I therefore supplemented it with the second part of my account: particulars, unlike properties, have criteria of identity. Those criteria are jointly the criteria of individuation, whereby one particular is taken to be numerically different from any others which are qualitatively identical; and the criteria of reidentification, whereby a particular is recognised to be numerically identical to a particular encountered on a previous occasion.

Fairly central in our conceptual scheme are those particulars which are physical objects, and I have already noted that other particulars are in one way or another related to physical objects themselves. The criteria of identity of physical objects essentially involve the spatiotemporal existence of those particulars. One table is numerically different from another qualitatively identical table if they occupy two different places at the same time: one table is numerically the same as a previously encountered one, even in a different place, if there is a series of adjacent spatiotemporal positions between its place then and its place now. So space and time, places and times, are intimately involved in the criteria of identity of physical objects. They are, therefore, also involved in the criteria of identity of all particulars whatsoever.[1]

One way to bring out this connection between particulars and spatiotemporality is to recognise that particulars are, by

their very nature, the possessors of properties – they appear in
propositions as subjects having properties predicated of them –
and that many of those properties are not simply 'monadic',
they are on the contrary *relational* properties relating two or
more particulars to each other. Big Ben is to the south of Ben
Nevis, for instance: 'to the south of' is a 'dyadic' relational
property relating the two particulars, Big Ben and Ben Nevis.
Ben Nevis is older than Big Ben: here 'is older than' is another
such property relating the same two particulars. The Battle of
Hastings happened between the founding of Rome and the
discovery of America; a *'triadic'* relational property 'happened
between' relates three particulars here (in this example the
particulars are events). And so on. Particulars stand in
relations of various sorts and various 'orders' (monadic,
dyadic, triadic and so forth) to other particulars.

We have looked already at one prominent kind of relation in
Chapter 4, the relation of causation. Relations which are
equally prominent in our world, and in our conceptual scheme,
are spatial relations and temporal relations. This, of course, is a
consequence of the fact that physical objects are themselves
central in that world and that scheme. Now physical objects
have the interesting feature that they, each and every one of
them, are related by spatial relations and by temporal relations
to every other physical object. There are, in other words,
spatiotemporal relationships between all physical objects: all
such objects have their positions in one spatiotemporal
framework. Moreover, since all other particulars can be themselves related in one way or another to some physical object –
John Smith's headache is something belonging to John Smith,
a physical object, and belonging to him at a particular time – it
follows that every particular can be said to have some
involvement with this single spatiotemporal framework.

Space and time figure therefore as categorial concepts in our
conceptual scheme. An account of these things must be given
which, at the very least, makes plain their connection with the
other categories, and I have already in the paragraphs above
given the general outline of such an account. One thing which I
have not yet settled is the question of their status in respect of
the categorial division between particulars and properties,
between substances and attributes, and this question is by no

means as simple as it might at first sight appear. Indeed, I think it fair to say that many of the debates over the nature of space and time which have figured so prominently in the history of philosophy have, in one way or another, reflected an uncertaintly over precisely this question. Many such debates can be seen to reflect a fundamental assumption that space and time are, or are not, particulars.

In Greek philosophy space and time were essentially treated as substances, particulars, and their nature seemed extremely elusive. Presumably the assumption was that if space and time were not *things* then they were nothing at all. But what things? One possibility, a position taken by some of the followers of Pythagoras, was that space could be equated with air. Another possibility was to treat space as a kind of container, a position taken by Lucretius and adopted by Plato in the *Timaeus*.[2] Time, too, seemed equally a substance of some kind, a flowing river, or in the view of the Pythagoreans, the whole of the universe itself – a view which Aristotle roundly rejected:

> Those who said that time is the sphere of the whole thought so, no doubt, on the grounds that all things are in time and all things are in the sphere of the whole. The view is too naive for it to be worth while to consider the impossibilities implied by it.[3]

Aristotle himself argued that time was best thought of as an attribute of attributes of substances, a measure of the movements which primary substances undertake: it is 'number of movement in respect of the before and after'. He was also aware of the kind of puzzle which seems to lead to the conclusion that time does not exist at all:

> The following considerations would make one suspect that it either does not exist at all or barely, and in an obscure way. One part of it has been and is not, while the other is going to be and is not yet. Yet time . . . is made up of these. One would naturally suppose that what is made up of things which do not exist could have no share in reality. Further, if a divisible thing is to exist, it is necessary that, when it exists, all or some of its parts must exist. But of time some parts have been,

while others have to be, and no part of it *is*, though it is
divisible. . . . Again, the 'now' which seems to bound the
past and the future – does it always remain one and the same
or is it always other and other? It is hard to say.[4]

Not all problems about space and time can be traced to this
question of their relationship to the category of substance,
however, and it must be admitted that many of the debates
over their nature were essentially of a kind which could be
settled only with further developments in the sciences. We will
look in a moment at the paradoxes of Zeno of Elea which
arguably needed advances in mathematical concepts
concerning infinite series for their solution. The question which
divided Leibniz and the followers of Newton, whether space
and time were absolute or relative, had at least an air of one
which could be resolved by science and not metaphysics.
However, it is now generally admitted that the Newtonians need
not have made the assumption of their absolute status since, as
Mach has argued, the notion of an inertial system which *is*
fundamental to Newtonian dynamics is definable in terms of a
relative notion of space and time after all. But questions
concerning the geometry of space, the relationship between
space and time, the nature of motion and so forth are treated in
the sciences in a way that no metaphysical investigation could
achieve. Modern physics takes the view that space is after all
not Euclidean in its geometry, and that the three dimensions of
space and the one of time are intimately related. Modern
physics too has seemed to show that nature has in fact provided
space with the kind of absolute distinction between clockwise
and anticlockwise rotation that Kant assumed was enough to
prove that space was absolute[5] – though it is questionable
whether it does establish Kant's conclusion. And the discovery
of the laws of thermodynamics, particularly in their
implications for entropy, has given some insight into the
physical foundation in nature of the anisotropy of time – its one
dimension of movement from past to future – and its connection
with the temporal direction of the cause–effect relationships in
nature.[6]

And yet the extent to which modern science can be said to
have solved the problems of space and time must be limited, in

that some of those problems are essentially problems in the field of categorial description. If we are puzzled by space and time it is often because we do not know how to fit them in with our other categories, and this is a question which science cannot answer for us. Are space and time particulars or properties? Are spaces and times, unique as each of them are in our spatiotemporal system, themselves particulars? Are spatial and temporal relations intrinsic to, *de re* essential properties of, the particulars that have them? These questions cannot be answered by modern physics, since they are questions about the manner in which we think about and talk about the world.

II. THE PARADOXES

In the history of the philosophy of space and time there have been a number of attempts to show that space and time are *unreal* – that is, that our experience of things in a spatiotemporal framework is an illusion. We can interpret these attempts as, at the very least, attacks on the concepts we have of space and time which involve the claim that there is something incoherent or self-contradictory about those concepts, and in consequence that reality cannot possibly be anything like those concepts depict it to be. Prominent among such attempts were, in Greek philosophy, the paradoxes of motion due to Zeno of Elea; and, in modern philosophy, the 'proof' of the unreality of time due to J. M. E. McTaggart. These two attacks between them have been responsible for a great deal of the metaphysics of space and time. The celebrated 'antinomies of pure reason' in Kant's *Critique* have, indeed, much in common with Zeno's arguments, and much contemporary philosophical debate over the 'myth of passage', the reality of time 'flowing' from past to future, has its origin in McTaggart's argument.

1. Zeno's paradoxes of motion
Zeno lived in the fifth century B.C., and followed Parmenides in holding that reality was unchanging. The paradoxes are designed to show that motion is impossible, at least on the assumption that finite extensions of space and time are made up of a finite number of spaces and moments. Other

assumptions about the nature of finite extensions being (in the current state of mathematics) inadmissible, the conclusion inescapably follows that motion is impossible.

The two most famous paradoxes of motion are the Achilles paradox and the paradox of the arrow. I will briefly outline them both before moving on to a longer discussion of McTaggart's argument. Zeno's paradoxes, in fact, required developments in mathematics for their solution, and represent the sort of metaphysical question which can only be answered by the scientist. McTaggart, on the other hand, produced an argument which science is powerless to answer.

Achilles and the tortoise

Suppose a race between the fastest man, Achilles, and a tortoise, a race in which the tortoise is given a head start. Zeno attempts to prove that Achilles can *never* catch up with the tortoise, and he argues as follows. At the start of the race Achilles is at point A and the tortoise at point B. In the time it takes Achilles to cover the distance from A to B the tortoise has moved forward a little to point C. Similarly, in the time it takes for Achilles to cover the distance from B to C, the tortoise has moved on to point D. Though Achilles comes nearer to the tortoise, he will *never* catch up. There is an unending, infinite series of stages like this which would in that case have to be covered in a finite time, and an infinite series of temporal stages cannot be contained in a finite time.

The arrow

Supposing an arrow in flight, Zeno attempts to prove that the arrow never moves. At any given moment the arrow is actually stationary in space, for insofar as it occupies a space which is identical in dimensions to itself it is not in motion within that space. Yet if the flight of the arrow is its occupying, at successive moments, successive such spaces then it is never actually moving at all.

I can do no better than quote Bertrand Russell's comments on these and the other paradoxes of motion:

Zeno's arguments, in some form, have afforded grounds for

almost all the theories of space and time and infinity which
have been constructed from his day to our own. We have seen
that all his arguments are valid (with certain reasonable
hypotheses) on the assumption that finite spaces and times
consist of a finite number of points and instances. . . . We
may therefore escape from his paradoxes either by
maintaining that, though space and time do consist of points
and instances, the number of them in any finite interval is
infinite; or by denying that space and time consist of points
and instances at all; or lastly, by denying the reality of space
and time altogether. It would seem that Zeno himself, as a
supporter of Parmenides, drew the last of these three possible
deductions.[7]

The invention of the infinitesimal calculus, and of the
mathematics of infinite series in general, allowed the
alternative solution of saying that a finite interval of space or
time could consist in an infinite series of points.

2. McTaggart against time

McTaggart's argument first appeared in 1908, in his paper
'The Unreality of Time'.[8] It begins with a commendable
account of the two ways in which we think about time, a
dynamic and a static way. The essence of the argument is that
the former, dynamic way of conceiving time involves an
ineliminable contradiction, and hence nothing can really exist
in time as we conceive it. Time, therefore, is unreal.

In more detail, and with my comments as the argument
proceeds, McTaggart starts from this claim: (i) *We think of time
in a dynamic and a static way, such that moments of time are conceived as
forming a dynamic series – the 'A series' – of past, present and future
moments; and a static series – the 'B series' – of moments earlier than, or
later than, other moments.* McTaggart sometimes seems to think
that these two series are series of *different* moments, when for
example he thinks of the A series as 'sliding along' the B series,
but that cannot be what he means. Rather, the *same* series of
moments must be the content of both A series and B series,
where the difference between the two rests on the relational
designations of those moments. Actually, he also uses the word

'event' to stand for the terms of the series, in a somewhat
peculiar manner:

> The contents of any position in time form an event. The
> varied simultaneous contents of a single position are, of
> course, a plurality of events. But, like any other substance,
> they form a group, and this group is a compound substance.
> And a compound substance consisting of simultaneous
> events may properly be spoken of as itself an event.[9]

I am not thinking so much of his use of 'substance' to designate
compound events, since I have suggested myself that events are
'substances'. I take his use of 'event' to be odd in that it is a
happening *at an instant*, and events are usually allowed longer
life than that. The division between events and processes is
somewhat arbitrary, and the former are not by any means all
instantaneous. Perhaps McTaggart's argument in the end
plays on an ambiguity over the sense in which an event can be
said to have duration, for he does see his instantaneous events
as having incompatible properties at different times of their
existence.

However that may be, McTaggart has certainly identified
two ways of thinking of time. The dynamic way is connected
with our use of tenses to refer to what *will* happen, *has* happened
and so forth; the static way with our dating system where the
relations of precedence and succession are involved. Which is
not to say that McTaggart claims, or would be right in
claiming, that tenses and a dating system are totally
independent: on the contrary, dating systems cannot work if we
do not know our own place in them, if we do not know where is
'now'.

McTaggart's next claim is this: (ii) *The B series is insufficient to
characterise time without the A series, which is therefore of fundamental
importance in our representation of time.* He argues for this in an
acceptable and an unacceptable manner. The former is his
argument that there are series like the B series, in involving
terms standing in transitive, asymmetrical relations, which are
not *temporal* series. An example would be the number series 1, 2,
3, . . . where each successive number is greater than its
predecessor. McTaggart gives as his example the meridian of

Greenwich, which passes through a series of degrees of latitude: what makes the B series temporal is that it is a series of *moments of time*, i.e. a series constituted by moments which change from being future, to being present, to being past – in a word, the A series.

The unacceptable argument simply begs the question. He argues the time is intimately connected with change, and change is impossible without the properties of past, present and future. The connection between time and change is put like this:

> In ordinary language . . . we say that something can remain unchanged through time. But there could be no time if nothing changed. And if anything changes, then all other things change with it. For its change must change some of their relations to it, and so their relational qualities. The fall of a sand-castle on the English coast changes the nature of the Great Pyramid.[10]

Ignoring the grossness of the assumption that time is *impossible* without change, and the peculiar Idealist monism of the Great Pyramid's changing nature, we should note at least that the kind of change McTaggart is talking about is a change in the properties of things like sand castles. These things change since at one moment they have a certain set of properties and at another moment a different set. But why should that imply that time is intimately involved with an A series as well as a B series?

Such changes are changes *in* time, and McTaggart needs to argue for changes *of* time to get to the A series. Indeed it is this latter kind of change which he (apparently illegitimately – given the quotation above) looks for in the B series and cannot find: it is only when we turn to the A series that we find changes which happen to moments themselves, changes *of* time:

> Take any event – the death of Queen Anne, for example – and consider what changes can take place in its characteristics. . . . In every respect but one, it is equally devoid of change. But in one respect it does change. It was once an event in the far future. It became every moment an event in the nearer future. At last it was present. Then it

became past, and will remain past, though every moment it
becomes further and further past.[11]

Moments, or 'events' as he calls them here, change only in the
A series, and since time is intimately connected with change it
requires the A series to exist. But what of the move from the
original change *in* time to this change *of* time, this 'temporal
becoming' as it is usually called?

Russell took the view that the A series was definable in terms
of the B series, since to say that a moment is past is to say that it
is earlier than this assertion; that a moment is present means it
is simultaneous with this assertion; and so forth. Change, for
Russell, was sufficiently accounted for as follows:

> Change is the difference, in respect of truth and falsehood,
> between a proposition concerning an entity and the time T,
> and a proposition concerning the same entity and the time
> T′, provided that these propositions differ only by the fact
> that T occurs in the one and T′ occurs in the other.[12]

Change is change *in* time, for Russell. McTaggart rejects this
line of approach with a passage that simply seems to beg the
question:

> I should, indeed, admit that, when two such propositions
> were respectively true and false, there would be change. But
> then I maintain that there can be no time without an A series.
> If, with Mr Russell, we reject the A series, it seems to me that
> change goes with it, and that therefore time, for which
> change is essential, goes too.[13]

I think that the best that can be said for this part of the
argument is that McTaggart has correctly pointed out that
there is a connection of sorts between time and change; that
change *in* time is arguably impossible without change *of* time
(the A series) because of the consideration about other
transitive, asymmetrical relational series mentioned above;
and that (tautologically) without change of the moments of time
themselves there is no 'temporal becoming', no A series.

There is just one more thing to note before going on to the

final, and most striking, move in the argument. This is that McTaggart is leading us to a position which involves ascribing various changing characteristics to moments or events *which do not exist*. A moment which has not yet been is said to be future, and one which has passed through the present is said to be past. Now events, on the normal notion of a (relatively) abiding particular, can have changing characteristics and present problems of reidentification just like changing particulars of other sorts. When it has ceased to be however, or not yet occurred, we do not usually allow it to have changing properties or any properties at all. This fact should make us hesitate to treat moments, or 'events' as McTaggart uses the term, as abiding particulars. They do not abide. Nor, actually, are two moments or 'events' ever qualitatively indistinguishable but numerically distinct; nor do we ever have to reidentify them as numerically the same as on previous occasions. Although they satisfy the Aristotelian requirement, if they are particulars they are limiting cases of that notion.

It seems that the A series characterisations of 'events' and moments which are *not* present have a rather peculiar status in our conceptual scheme. The sense in which a moment can actually *now* be *past* is not at all perspicuous. Of course, viewing the history of the world as a B series of moments or 'events', taking a God's eye view of things, allows us *from that perspective* to make use of the usual kind of criteria of identity for particulars. We *can* distinguish numerically distinct but qualitatively identical moments, in their various relations to other moments which happen earlier or later than they do; and we can find room for a notion of reidentification too. Working as it were with a spatial analogy, time becomes suited to our categories of particular and property and they to it. Perhaps it would be too much to claim that the A series perspective on time does *not* fit those categories, since after all there is an intimate link between the dating of events and our knowledge of our own place *now* within the system. And there is, too, a comparable problem about how to construe the spatial demonstratives 'here', 'there', and 'somewhere else', and *their* relationship to the map of space which we use. What is implied by this is, at least, that the A series (and its spatial counterpart) is apt to provide category puzzles and in consequence to lead us into paradoxes.

And this is exactly what happens in McTaggart's final step of his proof that time is unreal – (iii) *The A series involves a contradiction, which is not eliminable without an infinite regress*. He writes:

> Past, present and future are incompatible determinations. Every event must be one or the other, but no event can be more than one. . . . But every event has them all. If M is past, it has been present and future. If it is future, it will be present and past. If it is present, it has been future and will be past.[14]

Suppose that M designates the 'event' or moment which is *now*. Then this event or moment is *present*, was *future*, and will be *past*. Incompatible properties are being ascribed to the event or moment.

Yet there seems to be an easy answer to this charge, which if not met will mean the immediate downfall of the A series way of conceiving of time. The easy answer is to point out that these incompatible predicates are only apparently incompatible, since they are possessed *at different times*. After all, there is no incompatibility between a leaf being green on one day and brown on another:

> It is never true, the answer runs, that M *is* present, past, and future. It *is* present, *will be* past, and *has been* future. . . . The characteristics are only incompatible when they are simultaneous.[15]

And now McTaggart thinks he can show that this answer is inadequate, since it quickly leads into an infinite regress. In brief, it involves postulating a *second* A series to overcome the incompatibility in the first A series, and since that second series will require the same treatment to overcome incompatibility in *its* event determinations, we have an infinite regress of A series. The incompatibility in the first series is therefore *not* overcome, the A series remains guilty as charged and time is unreal. In McTaggart's own words:

> Our first statement about M – that it is present, will be past, and has been future – meant that M is present at a moment of

present time, past at some moment of future time, and future at some moment of past time. But every moment . . . is both past, present, and future. And so a similar difficulty arises. . . . If we try to avoid this by saying of these moments what had been said previously of M itself – that some moment, for example, is future, and will be present and past – then 'is' and 'will be' have the same meaning as before. . . . And so on infinitely.[16]

And he sums up the argument like this:

Such an infinity is vicious. The attribution of the characteristics past, present, and future to the terms of any series leads to a contradiction, unless it is specified that they have them successively. This means, as we have seen, that they have them in relation to terms specified as past, present, and future. . . . And, since this continues infinitely, the first set of terms never escapes from contradiction at all.[17]

McTaggart's argument is impressive, and none too easy to fault. Many have tried, and there is little agreement between them.[18] What lies at the heart of the argument is, I believe, a confusion over the categorial status of moments in time viewed in accordance with the A series, and associated with that a confusion over the categorial status of being present, being past, and being future. Are these two things substances and attributes, particulars and properties? It is not at all easy to locate them in the categories of substance and attribute, and that seems to explain the difficulty philosophers have felt in perceiving the faults in the argument, as well as being what the argument relies upon.

Let us start by noticing two things about McTaggart's reasoning. He argues, as we have seen, that present, past and future are incompatible predicates; yet they are not all possessed at the same time, but at different times. That admission, McTaggart thinks, is enough to get the infinite regress going since it is tantamount to postulating a *second* A series.

It is not. Rather, it is to revert to the B series conception of time, the vantage point from which all time is laid out before us like space. To say that M *will be* past in relation to some future moment is no more than saying that M occurs earlier than some other moment which is itself future. This, with a residual and unproblematic reference to the futurity of the postulated moment that is the point of comparison, is to conceive of the unchanging temporal relation of 'earlier than'. What is more, even though another series has been introduced, it is a series of the *same moments* but viewed statically. A series and B series are in that sense not different series of moments, only the same series viewed differently.

Secondly, there is no threatening incompatibility of predicates in the B series. Saying that M is past in relation to N is saying no more than that M is earlier than N. Saying that M is future in relation to O is saying that M is later than O. M can quite happily be earlier than N and later than O.

Why did McTaggart make these mistakes? In the first place, it is because of his strange notion of an 'event', which is all that is 'happening' at a given moment of time. 'Events' and moments are interchangeable throughout the argument. But 'event' is *not* equivalent to our notion of an event, which undoubtedly *does* have duration and hence can have incompatible predicates just like the leaf. Our events are particulars, substances, that can gain and lose properties. McTaggart is being misled by his strange notion of an 'event' to treat moments of time as themselves substances. In consequence, too, he is led into the absurdity of thinking that *dating moments* makes sense. Moments can, of course, be 'dated' in the B series conception of time, but that is no more than to say that the B series involves a series of dates, points in time: one cannot put a date on a point in time except in the sense of a numerical appellation. Events can be dated, but 'events' cannot, since 'events' are equivalent to moments. Events begin at a time, have duration, end at another time; moments do not *have* duration, and certainly have no moment of their beginning or being.

Associated with this miscategorising of moments is a failure to properly construe the status of being past, being present, and being future. 'M is past in relation to now' is a confusing locution, which suggests that being past is a property which M has now acquired. Moment M, apparently, can go through life having and losing the properties of futurity, presentness and pastness, but still exist for all that. But this is quite unacceptable. Being future, present and past are no more properties of things than being possible or impossible are properties of a world. 'The past' hardly consists of those actual moments of time which share the property pastness, any more than the possible or impossible consist of those actual worlds which share the property of possibility or impossibility. Such confusions are a consequence of treating what are not properties as if they were.

Of course, if M is earlier than N then M and N *do* stand in a certain temporal relation: there is no objection to treating B series relations as relations, even though they relate 'frozen' moments or dates in time. In that spatial perspective on time, we can talk of discriminating and reidentifying different moments. We can move around in time, in thought at least. So 'earlier than' is a relation and 3 o'clock on 3 February 1986 is a particular. But a moment in the A series is not a particular, and 'now' is not a property.

III. ABSOLUTE OR RELATIVE?

McTaggart's 'proof' of the unreality of time depends, then, in the final analysis on the obscurity of the relation between time and the categories of substance and attribute, particular and quality. More obviously, the debate in the seventeenth century between Leibniz and the Newtonians, on the issue whether space and time are absolutes in themselves or merely sets of relations between things, was a debate over the status of space and time as particulars or qualities.

1. Leibniz and the Newtonians
I said earlier that this debate – as contained in the exchange, for example, between Leibniz and the Newtonian Clarke[19] – had at least the air of one resolvable by science. It was indeed thought by Newton himself that there was experimental evidence for the existence of real, absolute, substantial space and time and so evidence to disprove the Leibnizian position that space and time were relative existents, relational attributes of things 'in'

space and time. This evidence however is insufficient for that
conclusion, and the decision really rests on considerations of
category description; the issue is really one of metaphysics, not
science. I will amplify this a little.

Leibniz was against postulating absolute space and time for
straightforward metaphysical reasons: he thought they were
inconsistent with his Principle of Sufficient Reason. On space,
he wrote this:

> Space is something absolutely uniform; and, without the
> things placed in it, one point of space does not absolutely
> differ in any respect whatsoever from another point of space.
> Now from hence it follows (supposing space to be something
> in itself, besides the order of bodies among themselves) that
> 'tis impossible there should be a reason, why God, preserving
> the same situations of bodies among themselves, should have
> placed them in space after one particular manner, and not
> otherwise; why every thing was not placed the quite contrary
> way, for instance, by changing East into West. . . . Their
> difference therefore is only to be found in our chimerical
> supposition of the reality of space in itself.[20]

He argued similarly against absolute time:

> Supposing anyone should ask, why God did not create
> everything a year sooner; and the same person should infer
> from thence, that God has done something, concerning
> which 'tis not possible there should be a reason, why he did it
> so and not otherwise: the answer is, that his inference would
> be right, if time was any thing distinct from things existing in
> time.[21]

Leibniz's own position was that space and time are attributes
of things, the systems of relations between spatial and temporal
existents, 'merely relative' to things themselves. Space he took
to be 'an order of things which exist at the same time', and time
'an order of successions' of things.[22] Putting a modern gloss of
his position, Broad comments that 'Leibniz regards space as a
logical construction out of places, and he regards a place as a
logical construction out of facts about the spatial relations of

bodies. And he holds that the notion of Absolute Space and absolute spaces is a fallacy of misplaced concreteness'.[23] So too for time.

Newton, on the other hand, argued for space and time being substantial things over and above whatever (if anything) occupies them. In his dynamics there figures centrally the notion of an 'inertial framework', a frame of reference with respect to which bodies move 'for which the minimum number of types of force have to be postulated in order to explain the motion of bodies'.[24] Now it is apparent that this notion is sufficient for drawing a number of distinctions which we might designate as 'absolute versus relative'. Firstly, if two bodies are moving with the same velocity within such a framework we can say that they have no 'relative velocity' but the same 'absolute velocity' within that frame of reference. Similarly we can designate their 'relative positions' which we can contrast to their 'absolute positions' within the framework – the first being constant, the second continually changing. And given these distinctions it is easy to construct similar ones between absolute and relative acceleration and rotation.

Interestingly, however, none of these notions of absolute position, velocity, acceleration or rotation require us to postulate absolute space or absolute time; none of them imply that we can make sense of the absolute position or change of position of a body in space and time quite independently of any given framework. Why should we think that it is necessary to go beyond our framework-relative distinctions? Newton's arguments for that step for space were drawn from what he took to be the real, experimentally observable effects of motion within absolute space, specifically of rotation around an axis.[25] One such example quoted by Newton is the oblate spheroidal shape of the earth which suggests that the earth is rotating around an axis which is fixed in relation to absolute space – the 'fixed stars' obviously fixed likewise in absolute positions in space. Another example is the variation in swing of a pendulum at the equator and at the poles, an effect again to be explained in terms of the rotation of the earth in absolute space. And a further example is the effect on the surface of water in a bucket which is swiftly rotated on a cord, where the water climbs upwards at the side. All these, thought Newton, provided evidence of absolute space, since they involved the effects of rotation within it.

In the nineteenth century, however, it was argued quite persuasively by Ernst Mach that absolute rotation is after all not observable. Newton's 'experiments' provide examples simply of rotation relative to the fixed stars, and who is to say whether there would be no centrifugal forces if the stars were rotated and the earth or bucket fixed instead?[26] Newton had after all provided no reason for claiming that absolute rotation had been observed, and hence for his notions of absolute space and time.

If the debate over the absolute or relative, substantial or relational nature of space and time is to be resolved it must therefore be, it seems, by metaphysics and not science. The Theory of Relativity has no obvious commitment to one or other alternative.

2. Kant's Transcendental Idealism

One consideration which made Kant favour the Newtonian position on space was an argument from incongruent counterparts.[27] Kant reasoned that space must be seen as an absolute, a substantial thing in its own right, as a condition of making sense of the distinction between clockwise and anticlockwise rotation. Suppose a lefthanded glove. All the points on that glove, such as the tip of the thumb and the tip of the index finger, can be described in their positions relative to all the other points, so a complete spatial description of the glove can be constructed. Yet, thought Kant, the same description would apply to a righthanded glove also, and in terms of relative locations of the various points on their surfaces it would not be possible to tell whether the description was of the lefthanded or the righthanded glove. Clearly, however, there is a spatial difference between the two since one could never occupy exactly the same space as the other – no matter how the second was moved around it could never be rotated into the space of the first. The space of the lefthanded glove is not therefore fully depicted by a set of relations between points on its surface, and it must be supposed that space is something over and above those relations.

It seems easy enough, however, to counter this argument

with the consideration that the difference between the left and right gloves could be fully described by an account of the relative positions of points on the surfaces of the two gloves together. In any case, it is not at all obvious that the conclusion that space is an absolute, a particular thing rather than a set of relations, follows from Kant's kind of consideration. In the event, Kant himself came to view the positions of both Leibniz and the Newtonians as incorrect, since they both took space and time to belong to things independent of the perceiving activity of sentient beings. In his *Critique of Pure Reason* he argues that they are, on the contrary, features of the phenomenal world for which we sentient beings are ourselves responsible.[28]

Kant is led to this conclusion, a major part of his theory of Transcendental Idealism, by considerations to do with the epistemological status of geometry and arithmetic. Briefly, he reasons that these two branches of mathematics constitute bodies of a priori propositions which are nevertheless informative, synthetic truths rather than trifling uninformative tautologies. How could we know such things a priori, though, if they were descriptions of the real world? How could we know a priori that in reality, for example, the angles of a rectilinear triangle add up to 180 degrees? If such knowledge is not of reality as it is independent of our experiencing it, but of features of our experience which the sentient mind has put there itself, then there is no mystery:

> If, therefore, space (and the same is true of time) were not merely a form of your intuition . . . you could not in regard to outer objects determine anything whatsoever in an *a priori* and synthetic manner. It is, therefore, not merely possible or probable, but indubitably certain, that space and time, as the necessary conditions of all outer and inner experience, are merely subjective conditions of all our intuitions, and that in relation to these conditions all objects are themselves mere appearances, and not given us as things in themselves which exist in this manner.[29]

Space and time, according to Kant, are 'empirically real but transcendentally ideal'. All things experienced by us are in

space and time, yet space and time are not themselves
properties of things in themselves beyond the reach of our
perceptual faculties.[30]

Kant's Transcendental Idealism can be countered by
questioning the assumption of this argument, that the truths of
geometry and arithmetic have the epistemological status which
he assigns them.[31] More to the point for the theme of this
chapter, it can be seen that Kant's new position has not greatly
clarified the status of space and time as particulars or
properties. On the one hand he is ascribing both space and time
to the sentient being as properties of that being itself, as features
of the manner in which objects are perceived. As such, they are
treated as ways of perceiving, not as particulars in their own
right. On the other hand, Kant wants to insist on their status as
things. In his 'metaphysical exposition of space', for example,
he insists that space is an 'intuition' rather than a concept,
meaning that it is a particular and not a concept which has
instances. His point could have been better put by saying that
the concept of space is the concept of a thing and not of a
property or set of relations, and the arguments are anything but
perspicuous:

> Space is not a discursive or, as we say, general concept of
> relations of things in general, but a pure intuition. For, in the
> first place, we can represent to ourselves only one space; and
> if we speak of diverse spaces, we mean thereby only parts of
> one and the same unique space. Secondly, these parts cannot
> precede the one all-embracing space, as being, as it were,
> constituents out of which it can be composed; on the
> contrary, they can be thought only as *in* it. Space is
> essentially one; the manifold in it, and therefore the general
> concept of spaces, depends solely on [the introduction of]
> limitations. . . . Space is represented as an infinite *given*
> magnitude. Now every concept must be thought as a
> representation which is contained in an infinite number of
> different possible representations (as their common
> character), and which therefore contains these *under* itself;
> but no concept, as such, can be thought as containing an
> infinite number of representations *within* itself. It is in this
> latter way, however, that space is thought; for all the parts of

space coexist *ad infinitum*. Consequently, the original representation of space is an *a priori* intuition, not a concept.[32]

IV. THE UNIQUENESS OF SPACE AND TIME

The last quotation from Kant's *Critique of Pure Reason* shows not only that he takes space (and similarly time) to be a particular, but that he takes it to be a *unique* particular. There are not two spaces but only one. True enough, there can be more than one space in the sense of a portion of space, but each such portion is a part of the one all-embracing space. And any stretch of time is but a part of the single, unique temporal series of the world. Space and time are *unique* particulars. To put it another way, all spatial and temporal things are spatially and temporally related to all other spatial and temporal things. Here, at least, Kant does seem to be describing a peculiar but indisputable feature of our conceptual scheme. Nevertheless it has recently been questioned whether this is also an *indispensable* feature of that scheme, or whether on the contrary we could make sense of more than one space or more than one time.

1. *Alternative spaces?*
The argument that space is not *necessarily* unique is advanced by Quinton on grounds a little more complex than the conceptual relativism which I will support in my final chapter. Quinton reasons that the essential features of space – that things in it are coherently organised and publicly available – could be retained even though its uniqueness had been lost.[33]

Quinton rightly points out that the mere conception of a spatial thing does not of itself imply that space is a unique individual. That a thing is spatial is either (i) its being extended, having parts spatially connected to one another, or (ii) its being spatially related to something distinct from itself. Neither implies that all spatial things are spatially connected. On what, then, does that thesis rest?

Quinton sees it as resting on the criterion of reality with which we operate, namely that something is real insofar as it is locatable in the one public and coherent space (and time).

There are, he admits, other spaces which philosophers have
often pointed out, such as Bradley's spaces of imagination,
dreams and fiction, and the empiricists' private visual fields.
Yet these other spaces lack the important characteristics of the
one physical space, on the one hand that things in physical
space are publicly locatable and on the other that they form a
coherent structure. 'Where the physical is vast and systematic,
the experiential is small and fragmentary; where the physical is
public, the experiential is private.'[34] It is precisely their
position in the public, systematic physical space which makes
things real for us.

Now given this criterion of reality the uniqueness of the space
of real things follows of necessity. However, and this is a crucial
and novel move in Quinton's argument, our having this
criterion of reality depends upon the *fact* that our experience
has the kind of systematic structure that it does have. It is
possible, says Quinton, to imagine our experience to be
different in such a way that it would be perfectly natural to say
that there is more than one space of real things, where this
means that there is no spatial connection between things in one
and things in other spaces. As this is so, we are not *forced* to
believe in the uniqueness of the space of real things and its
present necessity as a consequence of our criterion of reality is
seen to be dispensable. He writes:

That we have a certain concept at all can often be explained
by referring to facts which might not have obtained. With
any one concept there may be a number of such explanatory
facts which can be arranged in some order of importance.
The essentials of the concept would remain if some of the less
important facts did not obtain and if, therefore, the
conventions that depend on them did not exist.[35]

Quinton constructs an elaborate story, a 'myth', to describe
the kind of experience which might lead us to such a shift in our
thinking. Suppose, he says, that your dream life undergoes a
remarkable change. Each time you fall asleep you dream that
you wake up in a hut at the edge of a lake, and the dream
continues with a coherent sequence of events constituting a day
in your life as a lakeside dweller. When you dream you fall

asleep in the hut, you wake up in the usual bed and engage in your normal daily activities. Though he sees various problems to do with such issues as the length of the lakeside day in comparison to that of your 'sleeping' period, Quinton thinks these can be satisfactorily answered so that the myth is a plausible story of a possible form of experience. It is important that the two salient features of our normal unique space are retained in this dual-space world: the objects in the dream 'space' are publicly observable, available to other inhabitants of the lakeside village, and form a systematic, coherent structure of spatial relationships.

Faced with such a change in our dream life, Quinton argues, you would most naturally be led to postulate two spaces of real objects. The spaces are two since there is no spatial relationship between any object in the normal world and any object in the lakeside world. Clearly the criterion of reality with which we normally operate must be dropped, but there is an alternative to hand which Quinton offers us:

> If, failing to find the scene of my coherent dream in ordinary physical space, we insist that it is, then, only a dream we are neglecting the point of marking off the real from the imaginary. Why, as things are, do we have this ontological wastepaper basket for the imaginary? Because, approximately, there are some experiences that we do not have to bother about afterwards, that we do not, looking back on them, need to take seriously. . . . Reality, I am suggesting, then, is that part of our total experience which it is possible and prudent to take seriously. It is, of course, because I am ultimately interpreting reality in this way that I can envisage dispensing with locatability in one physical space and time as a criterion of it.[36]

How should we assess Quinton's argument, persuasive as it undoubtedly is in parts? Has he made out a case for saying that we are not compelled to think of space as a unique particular? Well, it is true that the concept of a spatial thing does not in itself involve that way of thinking. It is also true that our concept of space is closely involved with the notion of things in space being publicly observable, having systematic con-

nections one with another, and being spatially related each
to the others – this last, of course, being the uniqueness of space.
We can also agree that Quinton's own criterion of reality is in a
way part of our thinking about space: after all, the things in
space *are* 'that part of our total experience which it is possible
and prudent to take seriously', since on the usual criterion of
reality they are precisely the things that are real. On the face of
it we must concede the argument and its conclusion.

But categorial relativism with regard to space is not really
established by Quinton's manner of argument. Even conceding
that our concept of space has all these features built into it, and
that some of them can be dropped retaining others, does not
imply that *our* concept of space will be left intact. The simple
point here is that Quinton can at best be allowed to have
provided a case for saying that a concept *rather like* our concept
of space might replace that latter in certain circumstances. He
has not shown that *our* concept can find more than one
application.

This is an objection in principle to a paring down move such
as Quinton's to any of our concepts, and as such does not go too
deeply into the case offered specifically for the concept of space.
The following criticism, however, does. Admitting the various
ingredients of the concept to be roughly as Quinton has
claimed, there is clearly a need to investigate the interrelations
between them before we can sensibly claim that some can be
disposed of leaving a concept of space intact. Take for example
the connection between the uniqueness of space and the
systematic connections between things in space. A multi-space
myth such as Quinton's offers us the picture of a fundamental
breakdown in the systematic nature of our experience. True
enough, system is preserved within the different 'spatial'
worlds but then so it might be within, say, an individual's
visual field over quite an extended period or even within a
dream. A simple multiplication of different spatial worlds,
extending Quinton's own myth, would bring out the point that
the uniqueness of space is closely associated with the *single*,
overall systematic nature of objective experience. Local system
is not enough to provide for experience of the real world,
only global system of the kind provided by the one spatial
realm.

If uniqueness and system are so connected, then perhaps so too are the public availability of things in space and the existence of a spatial route from each thing to all the rest. The case is not easy to argue, but might be made plausible by emphasising the notion of experience of an *objective* world, such experience being one which contains nothing which intrinsically is available only to some observers. If I can get to an object in a place which is intrinsically inaccessible to you, that object and that place are not part of the objective world but of my private experience. It is then at least plausible to say that spatial routes always must be available to every observer of an objective, real world; and so, too, that the uniqueness of space cannot be dropped where the notion of a public world is maintained.

There is another question along such lines which Quinton never addresses, yet which concerns a fundamental feature of our category of the unique spatial particular. We do indeed think of space as a thing, a particular or substance, and moreover as a unique thing of its kind. The question is, if we adopted a multispace conception of our experience would that threaten not only our thinking of space as unique but also as a particular? If space were not unique, would the category of substance apply to it? Before answering this question I will turn briefly to the issue of the uniqueness of time.

2. Alternative times?

Though, as we have seen, he believes we can make sense of a dual-space experience, Quinton has reasons for saying that a comparable dual-*time* experience is not possible. His argument is prima facie a powerful one. What we would need to describe a multitemporal myth is, he says, 'two groups of orderly and coherent experiences where the members of each group are temporally connected but no member of either group has any temporal relation to any member of the other'.[37] But all these experiences, to constitute a dual-time experience as such, must of course be capable of figuring in my memory: if, say, either of the two groups were never remembered during the time the other group of experiences was being lived through, there would be no overall experience of a dual-time world. Now herein lies the insuperable difficulty, since if an experience is remembered by me then it *is* after all temporally related to the present:

> From the fact that, at a given time, I am logically capable of remembering a certain experience, it follows that the experience is temporally antecedent to the given time, the time of my current experience, and so is in the same time, the same framework of temporal relations, as it is. Thus if an experience is mine it is memorable and if it is memorable it is temporally related to my present state.[38]

It does appear that the search for a dual-time world myth is doomed because of this simple consideration. However, an attempt has been made to modify the description of the quarry by Swinburne in such a way that this objection is circumvented.[39] What if, Swinburne asks, we look for a myth involving two groups of orderly and coherent *events* – rather than experiences – where the members of each group are temporally connected but no member of either group has any temporal relation to any member of the other? In other words, what if we drop the requirement that we are to describe a dual-time experience of one person, but instead describe a dual-time world *simpliciter*?

Suppose, says Swinburne, a land occupied by two warring tribes A and B. To bring peace to the land, a seer causes each tribe to disappear from the sight of the other tribe, which then continue to occupy the land. After some time, since the experiment fails as each tribe starts to quarrel among itself, the seer reunites the two and things are as before. Here is a myth, thinks Swinburne, which describes a dual-time world. The times of the two tribes A and B are disconnected in the relevant way, no happening in A's world being at the same time as, before, or after any happening in B's world during their enforced separation. Why not? Because, says Swinburne, the place of these events is the same, and if they occurred say at the same time they would be observable by any observer at that place:

> . . . whatever occurs at the same place and at the same time as another event would, if it is the sort of thing such an

observer observes (viz. the observer must have and use the senses and the categories appropriate to observing the event), be observed by any observer of the second event. Yet this, *ex hypothesi*, does not occur.[40]

We might level our criticism again that such considerations hardly show *our* concept to have more than one application, but on the contrary simply introduce an alternative concept which retains some of the features of ours. This criticism might even seem to have more force here than in connection with the concept of space, since Swinburne readily admits that his concept of time disposes of the transitivity of temporal relations. An event in the solitary life of the A tribe is of course temporally related to all events before the act of tribal separation and all the events after the act of reconciliation, but then the same is true of an event in the solitary life of the B tribe. If we say that temporal relations are transitive we are thereby committed to a temporal relationship existing between these A and B events themselves, and the myth of dual temporality collapses. (So, presumably, does Swinburne's thesis that an observer must in theory be able to perceive two events taking place at the same place at the same time.) The myth therefore assumes a concept of time which does not involve such transitivity. Our reaction to this might quite naturally be that since such our concept of time involves it, and there could hardly be a temporal *series* without it, we cannot find his myth intelligible as a description of a multitime world. Dropping the transitivity of temporal relations is tantamount to moving away from time as such to a quite different concept.

Whether that is a large move is arguable, of course, and the argument would turn on the centrality of transitivity to our concept and whether the other main features of our concept have been retained. Quinton's features of the systematic connectedness and the public observability of events might be claimed to have been retained, so possibly all that is really essential to our concept of time is still there. Again, however, is that really so? There is a need to investigate the connections between the uniqueness of time and these other features before we can say that they can be retained when uniqueness has gone.

Take the systematic connections between things and events

which our temporal framework provides. Apart from the obvious worry that this system is grossly undermined by the lack of transitivity of temporal relations, a multitime myth offers a picture of a fundamental breakdown in these systematic connections. A kind of system is there, true enough, within the different 'temporal' worlds but then so it might be within a dream or within the confines of a novel. A multitime world loses the system provided by our unique temporal framework and replaces it with the poor substitute of local but disconnected, disjointed periods of events. The *real* world, the world of objective experience, enjoys an overall systematic temporal framework, and local system is not enough to provide for experience of reality.

And, once more, it is not just that uniqueness and system are closely connected: the public nature of events in the real world is intimately related to the existence of a temporal route from each of them to all the rest. Experience of an objective world is one in which everything is intrinsically available to all observers; so if I can get to an event which is intrinsically inaccessible to you, that event and the time of its occurrence are not part of the objective world but only of my private experience. Temporal routes must always be available to every observer of an objective, real world, and a multitime myth such as Swinburne's is tantamount to dropping the notion of objective experience.

We can conclude, then, that uniqueness is hardly a peripheral feature of our concept of time any more than it is of our concept of space. Its connections with the systematic and public nature of objective experience are such that the attempt to describe a multitime myth cannot succeeed. Changing our concept of time by disposing of uniqueness is changing a good deal of our conceptual scheme. Perhaps it involves, too, a shift of our concept of time away from the category of substance.

V. SUBSTANCES OR ATTRIBUTES?

I have argued in the present chapter that, insofar as the problems of space and time are not soluble by scientific procedures, those problems have an intimate connection with the question of which of the two categories of substance or attribute to apply to them. This was most obvious in the case of the debate between Leibniz and the Newtonians, though I argued at some length that the same was true of McTaggart's attempt to prove the unreality of time. I have suggested too that the question whether there can be more than one space or more than one time has its connection with this issue.

An adequate description of our categories of space and time must obviously be clear on the difference between spatial and temporal relations, spaces (places) and times, and space and time as such. How do the categories of substance and attribute apply to these different things?

Spatial and temporal relations are the easiest to handle here. Clearly they are not substances, not particulars in their own right but paradigm cases of attributes, properties of particulars. If A is to the left of B, then A and B are related by the attribute 'being to the left of', and it is definitive of attributes that they can be instantiated in other circumstances. If C is also to the left of D, the *same* attribute is found there. Similarly, if E happened before F, E and F are related by the attribute 'happened before', an attribute which can be instantiated in other circumstances. Spatial and temporal relations are not substances but attributes.

Spaces – or rather places, locations within space – and times, locations within time, are not so easy to categorise, for the reasons which I tried to spell out in my discussion of McTaggart. We have, I believe, a certain conception of space and time which makes no use of indexical terms like 'here', 'there', 'now' and so forth: on that conception, it is not too difficult to see how our category of particular can be made to fit locations within space and time. That conception involves a kind of bird's-eye view of spatial and temporal positions, which allows us at least in thought to move around within the framework and hence to be faced with the problems of identification and reidentification of places and times. On the other hand, the conception of space and time which does involve indexicals, McTaggart's A-series conception of time and a comparable one of space, does not lend itself so readily to the application of the category of particular to places and times.

What of space and time themselves? If the history of the

problems of space and time tell us anything, it is that we do have a strong tendency to subsume them under the category of substance, that is we do treat them as particular, individual things. Are there reasons why we should not do so? Well, to be properly subsumable under that category they must have the two features which we have discovered pertain to particulars in general. They must be such that they are never predicated of anything else though things can be predicated of them. And they must have peculiar criteria of identity, whereby it is possible to distinguish quantitatively distinct but qualitatively identical individuals of the same kind, and to reidentify them among that kind as 'the same as before'.

Now space and time, in our thinking of them, certainly do satisfy the first of the two requirements: we never predicate space or time of anything else, though we predicate many properties of them. They do *not*, however, satisfy the second of the two requirements, for the simple reason that they are unique individuals which have no peers. We are not called upon, for reasons which we have gone into, to distinguish say between two qualitatively identical but quantitatively distinct times as such, and so we have no need either to draw up criteria of reidentification. Are we to say therefore that space and time are after all not particulars?

To do so would be to refuse to allow any unique particular that status too, and that must be too high a cost. There are numerous kinds of things which, for one reason or another, have only one instance. God, in traditional metaphysics, has standardly been seen as such: more mundane examples would be the first woman prime minister of Britain, the first cuckoo in spring heard in Devon in 1986, and the tallest ever mountain. All these things to be sure are examples of larger kinds which do have more instances – Mrs Thatcher is a particular subsumable under the larger kind prime minister of Britain. But then, why can the same not be said of space and time? After all, space and time themselves have certain similarities and can be said therefore to fall under the same kind. We noted, too, that the temporal series has similarities to the progressive series of numbers, and to a series of points along a straight line. We must conclude that the fact that no qualitatively *identical* things can be found for space or for time does not disqualify them from being particulars. Our understanding of the contrast between substances and attributes must reflect this fact.

Finally, if we had found it possible earlier to countenance alternative spaces and alternative times, it is at least plausible to say that that would in itself have led us away from the category of particular to that of attribute. Space and time would have been seen as systems of relations which, like all relations, can be instantiated in more than one circumstance. This is not to say that all particulars must be unique: that would be more absurd than denying the possibility of unique particulars at all. Rather, the change would be a natural consequence of the motivation for recognising alternative spaces and times, namely that a system of relations of the proper kind is sufficient for calling our experience spatial or temporal. If we stress the system, we have no need to look beyond it for a particular, substantial space or time; if we stress the substantial nature of space and time, we are apt to treat them as unique.

CHAPTER 6   METAPHYSICAL TRUTH

I. REVIEW OF DISCOVERIES

The discussions we have been through, since Chapter 1, have been in the spirit of categorial description. The questions were addressed as questions concerning general and relatively fundamental features of the conceptual scheme we have for thinking and talking about the world, and no assumptions were made as to whether reality does itself closely correspond to that conceptual scheme, or whether that conceptual scheme is, in its more fundamental respects, the only one which we could have. These issues I now want to look at more closely, and in particular I want to raise the question whether categorial description can remain aloof from a commitment to metaphysical realism or metaphysical absolutism. First, however, I will summarise the results of these last four chapters as exercises in categorial description.

I have taken as relatively fundamental concepts, and hence as categories, those of substance, accident, cause, space and time. These categories exhibit many close connections, it really not being possible to give an adequate description of any one of them in total isolation from the others. Their connection can most simply be brought out like this: our conceptual scheme, in its most general and fundamental features, concerns particular substances which have accidents, and which stand in various relationships to each other, the most general and common being causal, spatial and temporal. There are other things in our conceptual scheme, such as people, societies and numbers, and arguably some of these should be included among the list of categories. There are other relations in which things stand to one another, such as those relations which persons have to other things like knowledge, belief, memory and expectation. But the categories singled out for treatment seem in many ways the more general and fundamental, though I will offer no argument of a Strawsonian or Kantian kind to establish that fact.[1] More importantly, a discussion of those favoured categories has provided a detailed and informative exercise in categorial description.

In Chapter 2 we looked at the category of substance, distinguishing the two Aristotelian notions, primary and secondary substances, and addressed these two notions as equivalent to those of individual or particular things and their kinds. It turned out to be quite difficult to arrive at a characterisation of an individual thing, and we traced a series of positions taken by philosophers on this question which exhibited clear associations and comparable failings.

Firstly, Locke's notion of the substratum of properties, the 'something we know not what' which together with those properties make up the individual, was found to provide an answer to a question which should not have been asked and to offer no assistance with the problem of individuating and reidentifying individuals. Two versions of the twentieth-century Logical Atomism theory of objects were looked at next, as a natural progression from Locke's substratum. We found that neither Wittgenstein's objects nor Russell's sensedata represented acceptable instantiations of our concept of an individual thing; and that the arguments put forward do not establish that our individuals, *via* the logical analysis of ordinary sentences about them into elementary propositions containing logically proper names, are 'logical constructions' out of those empiricists' objects. Leibniz's theory of monads also exhibits some of the failings of empiricism, and his thesis that particular things are instantiations of complete notions is unacceptable in its implications for the status of contingent propositions about particulars. The recent theory that names are rigid designators brings with it the claim that particulars have certain of their properties necessarily, and have them therefore not just in the actual world but in all possible worlds. Against this theory it was possible to find arguments suggesting that names are used to refer to things in the actual world, a background of historical knowledge being shared by their users, and that possible worlds therefore not only do not figure in our use of names for particulars but are themselves questionable entities.

Saying what particulars *are* required finding a way of distinguishing them from properties (this involving the contrast between particularity and generality) and finding a way of characterising the relationship between particulars and events. The final version of my description of this category involved two parts, one drawn from Aristotle's thesis that particulars cannot occur in the predicate position in a proposition, the second that particulars have criteria or principles of individuation and reidentification whereby they can be distinguished from other qualitatively identical yet numerically distinct particulars and recognised as numerically the same as those previously encountered. Events turn out on this account to be themselves a kind of particular, with their own definitive criteria of identity.

Chapter 3, on the topics of essence and accident, began with an assertion of the implications of this account for accidents or properties: their distinguishing mark is that they *do* appear in the predicate position in propositions as well as the subject position; what is more, they do *not* have criteria of identity since there cannot be two numerically distinct but qualitatively identical properties. This latter point entails that since natural kinds are really a species of property – even though Aristotle called them 'secondary substances' – natural kinds have no criteria for their individuation and reidentification. Of course individuals fall under natural kinds, and they have therefore such criteria which reflect in part the kinds which form their species; but kinds themselves lack the definitive features of individuals. There cannot be two numerically distinct but qualitatively identical kinds.

A longlived philosophical tradition, recently resurrected by Kripke, Putnam, Plantinga and others, allows for a division of accidents into those which are possessed contingently or accidentally and those possessed necessarily or essentially. The sort of necessity involved here is said to be *de re* rather than *de dicto*, and in its current form this tradition explains *de re* necessity in terms of truth in all possible worlds. The thesis that names are rigid designators already rejected in the previous chapter is an illustration of the idea of essential properties, those possessed by particular things in all possible worlds. Natural kinds are said to be another example of things rigidly designated by their names, a position which not only fails to allow for a difference in the function of names for individuals and the property terms standing for natural kinds, but also commits the Platonic error of treating kinds as particulars and looking for their criteria of identity. These are of course found in the essential properties of natural kinds, which Kripke sees in effect as Locke's 'real essence' properties. Against this theory I argued that our use of natural kind terms is to pick out kinds in the actual world, and that is against the background of our understanding of the natural laws governing the relationships between all the various properties of particulars which they possess as falling under different natural kinds. That we have such an understanding is ground enough to reject, too, Locke's account of natural kind terms as wedded to the 'nominal essence' of those kinds.

The chapter on causation addressed one of the most general types of relationship holding between particulars, one of the Four Causes recognised by Aristotle – the remainder were considered not to be categorial, or not as fundamental as efficient causation. The major dispute since the seventeenth century has been whether the causal relation involves a necessary connection between cause and effect, Locke's position being that it does so even though he distanced himself from the scholastic view which took such connections to be knowable a priori. Indeed, Locke thought that the necessary connections in nature would forever remain unknown, though were we ever to know the real essences of substances we could then see a priori that, since an event of one type has happened, an event of another type *must* follow. Empiricism has, since Locke, refused even this much room to the a priori in the necessities of nature; but Hume went further and disputed the presence of necessity altogether in causal connections, its presence having been misleadingly projected onto nature by the mind itself. These positions of Locke and Hume are represented in current thinking by on the one hand Harré and Madden, with their theory of the causal powers of particulars, and on the other by Mackie, who analyses causes as INUS conditions and takes the appearance of the necessity of causal connections as a reflection of our counterfactual thinking about those connections.

It is generally agreed that counterfactuals form part of our thought and talk about causal relations, and an analysis of these is required for an adequate characterisation of that category. This analysis proves to be one of the most difficult exercises in categorial description, and I looked at two theories which could be seen in their own way to represent the Hume–Locke controversy. The Humean position is taken, as just noted, by Mackie among others, and it treats counterfactuals such as 'If kangaroos had no tails, they would topple over' as disguised arguments with suppressed premisses. There are problems to be overcome by such an approach, but I suggested that those problems are not on the face of it insurmountable. Lewis is of the opposite opinion, and offers a Lockean account as an alternative to what he (I think inaccurately) dubs this 'metalinguistic approach'.

Lewis gives an analysis which rests once more on the notion of possible worlds which surfaced in Kripke's discussion of names and natural kind terms. The machinery of the analysis is impressive and the use to which possible worlds are put in this case is perhaps closer to their modern origin in modal logic. The counterfactual is given truth conditions which are such that it is true if and only if the corresponding material conditional 'Kangaroos have no tails $\rightarrow$ kangaroos topple over' is true in the closest antecedent-permitting possible worlds. Apart from having such unacceptable implications as those we noted for propositions about ideal gases, perfectly smooth planes and so forth, this approach suffers with others of its kind from the general dubiousness of the notion of possible worlds. Lewis takes a strongly realist line on these, in contrast to Kripke, and stumbles over such problems as the transworld existence of individuals and the claims of *im*possible worlds for equal recognition. Fundamentally, however, the Lewis approach lacks plausibility as a description of our thinking and talking about the world since the alternative 'metalinguistic' approach makes reference to things which undoubtedly do exist, namely our activities of proposing hypotheses and drawing inferences from them.

Chapter 5 discussed the other form of relationship between particulars which I call categorial, spatial and temporal relations. Not all particulars have a straightforward spatial existence since among particulars we have to include things that happen in the mental sphere for example, yet they are all associated one way or another with particulars which do have a spatial existence such as persons. It was shown in Chapter 2 that particulars have criteria of identity which involve spatial and temporal relations, so we could conclude that particulars have each of them an intimate connection with space and time.

We looked at the problems concerning space and time which the Greeks made so much of, including Zeno's paradoxes, and a more recent attempt to prove that time is unreal by McTaggart. The benefits of such discussions were a better characterisation of spatial and temporal relations, rather than an insight into unreality. We looked too at the debate between Leibniz and the Newtonians on the question whether space and time are absolutes or sets of relations, and at Kant's thesis that both space and time are 'empirically real but transcendentally ideal'. More recent debates on the question whether space and time are unique, or whether on the contrary our concepts of space and time allow for the possibility of more than one space or more than one time, permitted us to become a little clearer in our characterisation of those categories. One result was that we could resolve the issue of the status of space and time as particulars or universals, an issue which lay behind the dispute over the absolute or relative status of space and time.

II. AN ARGUMENT FOR CONCEPTUAL REALISM

I come now to the question whether the minimal metaphysical exercise of categorial description can in honesty remain minimal, whether it can remain aloof from any stand on metaphysical realism or metaphysical absolutism. So far its minimal status has been assured by an insistence that *all* that is involved is the correct characterisation of the fundamental features of thought and talk about reality, and the assumption that such characterisation need not be seen as one of reality itself, as required by metaphysical realism, nor as a characterisation of the only possible way of thinking and talking about reality as required by metaphysical absolutism. I want to offer an argument now to the conclusion that the first of these assumptions is a mistake, since a description of our categories *is* a description of reality itself; but the nature of the argument I will offer is not such as to commit categorial description to metaphysical absolutism. The position this leaves us with can be called 'conceptual realism', and I will work towards my argument for this kind of metaphysical realism by looking at an attempt by David Hamlyn to link facts with the notion of what people agree to be the case.[2]

1. A Wittgensteinian line

If Hamlyn is right, and general agreement makes the facts in the world, then the connection between categorial description and metaphysical realism is easy and direct: people agree in their thought and talk about what there is, hence a description of this practice is a description of reality. What is more, room is left for the practice to change over time so metaphysical absolutism is ruled out. It is important therefore to see why the connections cannot be so easily made.

Hamlyn's argument takes off from some central thoughts of Wittgenstein's published in the *Philosophical Investigations*, in particular his claim that 'an inner process stands in need of outward criteria'[3] and the cryptic comment numbered 242:

> If language is to be a means of communication there must be agreement not only in definitions but also (queer as this may sound) in judgments. This seems to abolish logic, but does not do so. – It is one thing to describe methods of measurement, and another to obtain and state results of measurement. But what we call 'measuring' is partly determined by a certain constancy in results of measurement.

In this quotation Wittgenstein is drawing a connection of some kind between public agreement and communication, and that might seem in theory wholly acceptable. If people do not agree on their use of language, how can there be any communication between them? But the rest of the quotation shows that more is at stake than this, and what more is given by his simple example. If there is going to be a practice of using terms for the lengths of objects, measurements such as 'two feet long' or 'greater than the other one', then this requires that people do in general agree on the results of an act of measuring an object. Without such agreement in results there is no chance of a practice of measuring to exist at all. So the quotation involves at least some agreement over the facts concerning length, for example, as a prerequisite of the language of measurement. And presumably Wittgenstein would extrapolate from there to a connection between language and agreement in a general way on what there is.

The other quotation, about inner processes, harks back to the discussion of the language we use for talking about people's pains, hopes, fears, thoughts and so on. His thesis, supported by the set of comments[4] known collectively as 'the private language argument', is that the practice of describing other people's inner processes – and one's own too, for that matter – presupposes that there are criteria for establishing their existence and nature; what is more, these criteria are public in kind, making use of features of behaviour and demeanour which are available for all to see. After all, how can there be public agreement if there are no public criteria of inner processes? When a man is in pain he exhibits this in characteristic ways, ways which are quite different from what he does when he is feeling content with life, anticipating a win on the horses, and so on.

It is important to note that Wittgenstein is using the term 'criterion' in a special way, a way which it has proved difficult to characterise in preexisting philosophical terms.[5] The relationship proposed between, for example, pain and pain behaviour is one which allows someone to feel pain yet not exhibit it and to exhibit pain yet not feel it. All that is required is that *normally* pain and pain behaviour go together, and such cases as these are abnormal. The notion of 'normally' used here is not equivalent to that of generally, a statistical notion, but one where the contrast is with something like 'where there are special reasons why not'. What is more, proponents of the Wittgensteinian idea of 'criterion' have resisted its explication in terms of the notion of inductive evidence, denying that pain behaviour is good inductive evidence for pain itself, presumably on the grounds that there is a conceptual connection here which goes beyond inductive evidence. In any case, to say that a certain kind of behaviour and demeanour is the criterion of pain is to say that normally when people exhibit that behaviour they are in pain.

Now Hamlyn generalises this use of the idea of a criterion, insisting that *every* concept needs such a criterion, not just those concerning inner processes.[6] Observational concepts such as colours require them too, red for example having the criterion 'looking red': normally if something looks red then it is red. The criterion must of course have the relevant kind of distance from the concept as well: something can look red yet not be red, and vice versa. The idea goes over to the concept of fact – and truth and objectivity, which are closely associated with fact. What criterion could there be for the concept of fact? The answer is, on Hamlyn's approach, general intersubjective agreement. Normally, if people agree on something it is true, it is a fact. Public agreement might not exist, for some special reason, on some particular facts, and public agreement might for some special reason exist where fact does not. Nevertheless, public agreement is closely attached to the concept of fact in a manner which goes beyond the merely inductive.

Hamlyn's conclusion seems to offer a powerful tool against the philosophical sceptic who questions our ability to know things about reality, as well as providing the link between categorial description and realism or absolutism. In fact it seems to be its implications for scepticism which primarily motive his argument. In this, however, it is soon obvious that it fails in its purpose, since the scope of the thesis is left unclear. What precisely constitutes the class of judgements which the thesis refers to? *All* judgements whatsoever which people make about *any* matters whatsoever, or limited classes of judgements such as those about the lengths of things, their colours and tastes, the inner processes of other people, the past, the future, aesthetic and moral issues, and so forth? Typically the sceptic questions our ability to achieve knowledge in one or other area of enquiry and the thesis would need to apply to each such area individually to silence him.

That Hamlyn intends it to apply only quite generally might be assumed from his attitude to the problem of scepticism about the past proposed by Russell's hypothesis, that the world might have come into being only a few minutes ago complete with all ostensible records and memories of a wholly unreal past. This seemed to Russell sufficient reason to question our ability to know anything at all about the past. According to Hamlyn[7] our general agreement on the facts about the past is *not* sufficient to establish that they are indeed the facts notwithstanding general agreement being the criterion of fact. In this case, he thinks, circumstances are abnormal since there is a special explanation of the breakdown of the connection – the miraculous origin of the world. Arguably this is the line which Hamlyn must take, keeping his thesis of very general application to judgements as a whole, otherwise he runs into the following problem: the general agreement over the spirits and demons which inhabit trees and rocks found in a particular culture would warrant the conclusion that there are indeed such inhabitants, that facts are as they are taken to be. Yet the sceptic is going to react, if Hamlyn's thesis is kept so general, that he has provided no grounds for rejecting scepticism in any particular area of enquiry and so missed contact with traditional sceptical worries.

Leaving to one side then the issue of scepticism, let us ask whether Hamlyn has put up an acceptable set of considerations for his conclusion. The first problem is his insistence on the generalised version of Wittgenstein's claim for criteria for inner processes: *all* concepts have criteria for their application. Not only is no support offered for this, it is a thesis which lacks plausibility on a number of counts. Firstly, it appears to lead to an infinite regress since every concept involved in the criterion for a given concept will need a criterion too. The concept of pain, for example, is provided with a criterion which involves a set of alternative descriptions of behaviour and demeanour the satisfaction of any of which normally ensures the existence of pain; but each description makes use of concepts which themselves require criteria for their application, such as 'clutching the stomach while emitting a moan'. In the case of terms like 'red' and 'sour', however, things are even worse since the criteria offered by Hamlyn involve those very terms themselves: the criterion of being red is looking red, and the very concept of redness appears in its own criterion. At least the regress is brought to an end but only, apparently, by means of an imminent circularity. Secondly, the concepts which concern inner processes present a different problem to those which concern publicly available phenomena such as colours and tastes, or even facts about them, and the connection between agreement in judgements and language which Hamlyn depends on argues only for criteria of a public kind in the case of inner processes. There is no warrant for extending Wittgenstein's claim to all concepts whatsoever from the demands made on language by inner processes.

Another reason for questioning Hamlyn's conclusion is that it rests squarely on the private language argument, and that in at least two ways. The basis for the notion of a criterion we have seen was that private language argument in the *Philosophical Investigations*, and we have questioned its generalisation to all concepts. But what is more Hamlyn is depending directly on the private language argument in his selection of the criterion of the concepts of facts, truth and objectivity. Why *public agreement*, we may ask, rather than some other phenomenon? What has intersubjective agreement got to do with fact, truth and objectivity anyway? True enough, the notion of objectivity implies that something is the case independently of one person's saying so, it implies the idea of that which is intersubjective and not just subjectively judged to be the case. Yet this in itself does not get us to intersubjective *agreement* in the sense of general acceptance of the fact in question, and that gap must be filled by some further consideration.

The answer seems to be that Hamlyn is relying upon the Wittgensteinian association between the use of language for communication and the agreement in judgements asserted in the second quotation: if language is to be a means of communicating, there must be agreement in judgements as well as definitions. But the implication of the private language argument is that all language is communicative since there cannot be a language, a private language, which could not be used for that purpose. It follows that there is a close connection between language *simpliciter* and agreement in judgement, and how better to express this conclusion than in the jargon of

criteria and say that agreement in judgements is the criterion of
fact, truth and objectivity?

Hamlyn's thesis rests therefore on Wittgenstein's notion of a
criterion and the associated private language argument. It falls
if these are rejected, and there certainly do seem to be powerful
arguments available which can be put up against the private
language argument in particular.[8] Since we have seen reason
too to question the notion of a criterion in Wittgenstein's sense,
and the generalised use to which Hamlyn has put that notion in
his argument, we cannot accept his thesis that public
agreement is the criterion of fact. The connection between
categorial description and metaphysical realism must be made
in a different way.

2. *Facts, concepts and categories*

The Hamlyn thesis might seem to have a certain air of
plausibility, however, when disentangled from its supporting
arguments, and as a way of starting my own proof of conceptual
realism I will remove those features of it which I think are
unacceptable. Hamlyn's thesis, then, is that public agreement
is the criterion of fact. The first thing which must be dropped is
the Wittgensteinian notion of a criterion, for the reasons we
have just seen, and this leaves us with a thesis asserting that
there is a connection *of some kind* between public agreement and
fact.

Let us note next that it is wholly implausible to suggest that
the thesis should read: public agreement is the necessary and
sufficient condition for fact. This follows, firstly, from the
consideration that there are (and are generally recognised to
be) many facts not only about which we do not have public
agreement but of which we have no inkling at all. Take for
instance the precise number of grains of sand on the British
coastline, or the distance at the moment between Big Ben and
the centre of the moon, or the nature of the human species in
fifty thousand million years from now, or how exactly the
inhabitants of Mohenjodaro in ancient India pronounced their
vowels. So public agreement cannot be regarded as a *necessary*
condition for fact in general, even though perhaps it is such a
condition for *established* fact and that only tautologically. But
secondly, public agreement is clearly no *sufficient* condition for

fact either, as there are many things about which public agreement has got it wrong. The shape of the earth, the number of planets in the solar system, the movement of the planets around the sun, are just some examples which can be added to quite easily. Public agreement, then, is neither a necessary condition nor a sufficient condition for a fact.

One inviting way to improve on that thesis is to replace 'public agreement' with 'publicly agreed criteria for establishing the facts', the satisfaction of which could then be said to be both necessary and sufficient for fact. Now if this has any hope of being right we must understand the notion of criteria here in a non-Wittgensteinian way, so that we are thinking of something like rules for carrying out investigations or rules for saying when something is the case, is a fact. It might of course be difficult to know whether the rules have been properly adhered to or whether the rules are totally satisfied in a particular case and hence difficult to know whether we are dealing with a fact; but these difficulties would be no more than a reflection of the general problem of certainty in knowledge claims. More importantly, if the thesis is to be believed the notion of these criteria being satisfied must be taken in the sense that their being satisf*iable* rather than their having actually been seen to be satisfied as such. If not, we are back with the problems of the last paragraph and are no further ahead. Let us then take the thesis to read: that there are publicly agreed criteria for establishing a fact is both necessary and sufficient for there to be a fact.

And now we must drop as well the requirement that these criteria be publicly agreed, since that too was a part of Hamlyn's thesis supported by the questionable private language argument. In defiance of that argument we can suppose that criteria for establishing what is the case, rules governing investigatory procedures and circumstances under which something is taken to be a fact, might well be possessed by one person alone. Of course, we can say, if language is to be a means of communication there must be agreement in definitions and judgements, so the individual must share his rules with others if he wishes to communicate with them. In the absence of such a wish there is no need for the rules to be publicly shared and so publicly agreed, and criteria *simpliciter* for establishing facts can therefore stand alone as the necessary and sufficient condition of fact.

We arrive almost at the premiss of my argument for conceptual realism: facts exist when criteria for establishing them exist, rules governing investigatory procedures and the circumstances under which something is taken to be a fact. There are facts, for example, about the number of tables in the next room and the number of rooms in the building since there are rules for counting, rules for individuating tables and rules for individuating rooms. In the absence of such criteria there are no facts to be established.

Before proceeding further I will note the relevance of a point made above to this thesis. There is a general problem of certainty which extends to the question whether such criteria have been satisfied, yet this creates no difficulties specific to this sort of knowledge. It might be difficult to establish that correct procedures have been followed or that circumstances really are such as they are taken to be, so that a mistaken conclusion is arrived at. Yet if they have, it follows that a fact has been established; if not, then a mistake has been made. It can, however, be no objection to an account of facts that it leaves room for mistakes about them. And another point which is connected to this issue must be noted too, that it may in particular cases be not only difficult to be sure that the criteria have been satisfied but actually impossible.[9] One reason might be that the procedures cannot be put into application in a particular case, such as counting the number of planets in the universe, and yet there is a definite answer and hence a fact which lies hidden from us. Another might be that normal procedures for establishing a fact make it impossible to establish another, such as the measurement of both velocity and mass of a microscopic particle, but arguably there are two facts nevertheless. Criteria for establishing facts need not then be infallibly applicable nor applicable in all cases where facts exist, and this must be understood as assumed by the premiss of my argument for conceptual realism.

Can criteria for establishing facts be both necessary *and* sufficient for facts? If they were sufficient then facts would be created simply by the creation of criteria for establishing them and that supposes too much control over reality by the human mind. At best the invention of criteria for facts is the invention of a set of rules which have then to be applied if the world provides material for their application. Whether it is a fact that there are three chairs in the room next door depends not only on the procedures of counting and individuating chairs and rooms, but also on the outcome of those procedures in the given case, which outcome cannot be preordained at the time of inventing the procedures. Criteria for establishing facts are necessary for facts to exist but not sufficient, since sufficient conditions involve the positive outcome of the application of those procedures. Here then is the thesis which forms the premiss of my argument for conceptual realism: criteria for establishing facts are a necessary if not a sufficient condition for facts to exist.

My proof proceeds as follows. These criteria have been taken so far to include two things, a procedure for pursuing the investigation and a rule governing the circumstances under which the fact is taken to exist, and these two things are intimately related. Indeed, the former is quite properly to be regarded as a direct consequence of the latter, for when the circumstances are known under which the fact is to be declared it is known too what kind of thing needs to be done to arrive at those circumstances. In the example of the number of chairs in the next room clearly a knowledge of what counts as a chair and what counts as counting chairs gives more than a hint as to what needs to be done to establish the fact. The example is easily generalised, and the implication is clear. A knowledge of what constitutes a given fact is itself a knowledge of the kind of investigation which will establish that fact, with the reservations expressed above about difficult or impossible cases. A necessary condition of a fact is therefore the existence of a rule governing when that fact exists.

Now what are concepts if not such rules? A concept is something which permits its possessor to see the world in a certain way, to recognise an instance of a kind when presented with one in reality or to conceive of one in thought. When someone has the concept of an F he knows one when he sees one, and can expect, hope for, imagine and contemplate an F too. Having the concept of a dog involves knowing what dogs are, and that brings with it all those skills. The conclusion follows that there are facts only when there are concepts, that concepts are in this sense generators of facts.

I conclude that conceptual realism has been established, in a form not specific to categories as such but covering all concepts whatsoever. A description of the concept of a table is therefore a description of tables, a description not just of thought and talk about reality but of reality too. A table, as we discovered in Chapter 2, is a physical object satisfying a certain functional description, and as a physical object it has a principle of individuation and a principle of reidentification which concern spatiotemporal location and movement through space and time. A description of this concept is a description of a kind of thing in reality, not just a way of thinking and talking about reality.

The individual, in generating his own set of concepts, is not completely inventing reality, since such a reality would involve all sorts of absurdities which match the logical inconsistencies and other incoherences in his concepts as well as satisfying each and every one of them. There clearly cannot be this kind of creativity in the human mind, and at best we can assert, so far as concepts in general are concerned, that we make the concepts and the world fills them in. A concept is a way of depicting what is there, and what is there is not given simply by the concept itself. Armed with our concepts we can see if there are things to fit them to; or rather, since that suggests that the things, entities, beings of the world exist before and beyond the concepts, armed with the concepts we see whether we can mould the world in terms of them. If we can, then there are facts for us to uncover.

But were there not facts before any concepts had been invented, before say the earth had cooled sufficiently for any animal life to emerge? And will there not be facts after all animal life has disappeared with the heat death of the universe? There is no reason to deny these claims, and what I have said is quite consistent with them. A conceptual scheme is applicable beyond the here and now, both backwards and forwards in time to things before and after its possession by any living thing. That is why we can talk of facts temporally far distant from us, and spatially too, and that is why we can say that there were facts about such things as the speed of light and gravitation before concepts covering them had been invented. A more difficult case for my thesis is presented by the idea that facts might exist which we have no concepts for at the moment, a plight which we no doubt share with previous generations and which each individual must suffer as his conceptual development proceeds. If there can be such facts without the corresponding concepts, how can I claim that concepts are a necessary condition for facts? I suggest that this is no real problem for that thesis, since an imaginative speculation about the possibility of kinds of facts not dreamt of in our conceptual scheme is at the same time a speculation about the possibility of concepts not included in it. Since concepts are necessary for facts there can be no facts without concepts. But since we can imagine there to be facts outside of our conceptual scheme we can therefore imagine there to be concepts to be invented and applied. This requires the recognition only that our conceptual scheme might well be inadequate, not that all concepts might fall short of the facts.

Conceptual realism applies to concepts in general, hence to the categories I have discussed in previous chapters. These are the most fundamental and general of all concepts in our conceptual scheme, standing to more specific ones like table and cat, battle and cyclone as presuppositions or partial contents of them. A cat, for instance, is a spatiotemporal particular which causally interacts with its environment, and the concept of a cat involves these categories too. Since there are cats there are things answering to our categories, and we could for that reason embrace metaphysical realism. I have argued for it from a different route, drawing the connections between concept and fact in a general way, showing that concepts are a necessary condition of facts existing and hence that a description of concepts is a description of reality. Conceptual realism being established in that manner, it is plain that categorial description itself is committed to metaphysical realism after all.

III. IMPLICATIONS OF CONCEPTUAL REALISM

Since categorial description is in the last analysis something more than a mere account of the fundamental features of thought and talk about reality it follows that the idea of metaphysical truth has greater content than was assumed in Chapter 1. There it was claimed that there are indeed truths to be discovered in metaphysics, and that these truths are empirical, factual ones about our ways of thinking and talking about the world. They have a problematic status only insofar as they share that with any truths about intentional phenomena, and metaphysical claims should be recognised as objective, cognitive claims on a par with claims about the contents of the next room. Certainly there are questions about the criteria for their acceptance with which we operate, but we do operate with some such criteria and we can adjudicate in terms of them between rival metaphysical claims, and what is more we can now see that those criteria themselves are not distinct from intentional concepts in general. Yet now we have admitted a commitment on the part of categorial description to metaphysical realism, must we revise this account of metaphysical truths?

1. Metaphysical absolutism

For most brands of metaphysical realism it would be true that metaphysical absolutism is presupposed. Clearly Aristotle's account of the fundamental species of being assumed that the truths of metaphysics were unchanging, since they were truths about an unchanging reality. Even Kant's non-realist account of metaphysical truths, those anyway concerning the categories of thought which men have for handling the world of experience, came with assumptions about their status as necessary truths and not just contingent ones. Kant shared with Aristotle, as we saw before, a belief in the non-relative, absolute nature of the results of categorial description. Only Collingwood's account of metaphysics as concerning the fundamental presuppositions of current science allowed for change and therefore a relative, non-absolute characterisation of metaphysical truth.

Conceptual realism is different. The peculiarity of

conceptual realism is that it takes facts to be in part, in important part, constituted by the concepts which are used to give structure to reality, and since conceptual schemes undoubtedly do change over time this makes room for change in the facts themselves.[10] Categorial description can then involve objective, empirical truths which yet have no absolute status such as other brands of realism have given them. From the point of view of conceptual realism there may well be alternative realities, since there may well be alternative conceptual schemes. Our thought and talk about reality has at its very centre provided for spatiotemporal particulars which stand in causal relationships one to another, and there are therefore such particulars in reality itself. On the other hand we have not explored such reasoning as offered by Kant and Strawson for the assertion that our conceptual scheme *must* have these features in it and in consequence the assertion that categorial description results in absolute, non-relative truths: yet such arguments would indeed be needed to supplement the claim of conceptual realism, since that brand of realism does not produce an absolutist conclusion on its own.

2. *Cognitivism*

One major advantage of the minimal activity of metaphysics, categorial description, was supposed to be its ability to avoid the standard charge of the anti-metaphysician that metaphysics engages in propounding claims which go beyond the bounds of any possible confirmation or disconfirmation by experience and which are in consequence lacking in empirical content. Such was the charge of the Logical Positivists[11] in the early part of this century, and such a charge lay behind Kant's rejection of speculative metaphysics as an area of endless controversy and an illusory pretence to knowledge.[12] Moreover, so the anti-metaphysician argued, the claims of metaphysics are supposed to be synthetic, and (with reservations lodged by Kant) the only way synthetic propositions can be established is by empirical means – there are no synthetic a priori propositions. The Positivists, Kant and Hume[13] together, would 'commit metaphysics to the flames' as lacking cognitive content, containing 'nothing but sophistry and illusion'. Categorial description seemed to avoid this attack, but now we see its own involvement with metaphysical realism does it still come away unscathed?

Yes it does, since its claims are of a factual, empirical nature. That our conceptual scheme involves the concepts I have singled out as categories is a fact which has to be discovered, and the evidence for it is the manner of our thought and talk about reality. That our categories in an important way constitute reality itself does not change this evidence, and categorial claims are still empirical, factual ones. But the same is true of those features of reality which are a reflection of the categories too: that reality contains spatiotemporal particulars which causally interact, that particulars differ from universals in that they have criteria of individuation and reidentification, and so on, these are things which we have to discover by attending to the relevant features of our thought and talk about reality and so are themselves empirical, factual truths.

Yet are they not conceptual truths, and so necessary rather than contingent? And being necessary, are they not a priori and non-factual? It is important to recognise that not all truths about concepts are conceptual truths, if by a conceptual truth is meant a necessary one. We discover empirically that our thought and talk have the features that they do, and so empirically that reality has them too. We might discover empirically (and pretty easily) that our conceptual scheme has in it the concept of a bachelor, a concept which involves that of being unmarried – and we discover that empirically too: it is nevertheless a conceptual, necessary truth that bachelors are unmarried, to be distinguished from the contingent truths about the concept that it is contained in our conceptual scheme and that it has the features that it does. The same holds true for the fundamental features of that conceptual scheme. That particulars have criteria of identity and universals do not is a conceptual truth and hence a necessary one; that our conceptual scheme involves such categories of particular and universal is an empirical, contingent one; that reality contains such particulars and universals is, since a consequence of their inclusion in our thought and talk about it, an empirical, contingent one also.

3. Essentialist metaphysics

If we say that metaphysical truths are empirical truths about the features of reality which reflect the fundamental concepts in our conceptual scheme, how should we characterise metaphysical falsehoods? I have argued against the recent trend towards essentialism in metaphysics, manifested in the work of Kripke on names and natural kind terms as rigid designators and in the theory of counterfactuals of Lewis, and such essentialist metaphysics I take to be a prime candidate for metaphysical falsehood. How is it false?

In the first place, essentialism constitutes an unacceptable description of the categories embedded in our thought and talk about the world, so an empirically false description of that thought and talk. Secondly, in consequence of the points argued in the last few pages, we can say that essentialism is a factually inaccurate, empirically false account of the features of reality which reflect our categories. It is not the case that there are *de re* essential properties possessed by the particulars in the world, it is not the case that there are *de re* essential properties possessed by the natural kinds in reality, and it is not the case that possible worlds exist as well as the actual one in all of which those particulars and natural kinds have the properties labelled essential. There are no *de re* essential properties, and there are no possible worlds, and both of those things are empirically, factually the case. Metaphysical falsehoods are at least unproblematic in their cognitive status.

Which is not to say, of course, that essentialist metaphysics does not contain necessarily false claims at all. It is a factual truth about the concept of a natural kind that a natural kind has no criteria of individuation and reidentification, that this is a feature of the concept of natural kind in our conceptual scheme; and in consequence it is a factual truth that reality has in it natural kinds which lack such criteria. At the same time, since the concept is like that, it is conceptually true and hence necessarily true that no criteria of identity exist for natural kinds. It is therefore necessarily false to claim, as essentialist metaphysicians do, that natural kinds do have such criteria. There is, again, no paradox here. The factual truths and falsehoods concern the nature of our concepts and, in consequence of conceptual realism, the nature of reality too; the conceptual truths and falsehoods are not about those concepts in the same way, since they are assertions which use those very concepts themselves.

Might essentialist metaphysics be offered as an improvement on the actual categories which we have at our disposal at present? Categorial description has been kept free of metaphysical absolutism by the argument establishing its connection with realism, and it is certainly not obvious that those categories are the best we could possible have. As essentialism becomes more widespread in its manifestations it inevitably appears to offer the most attractive way of holding together the otherwise diverse categories of our thinking and talking. That of course is a self-sustaining illusion, powerful though it undoubtedly is. Once recognised to lack this advantage in truth and reality, it is open for us to judge essentialism on its real merits. Then attention can turn to questions such as whether the notion of a possible world is a coherent one, whether it contravenes the demand for simplicity contained in Occam's Razor, and whether it can be pressed into service as the various manifestations of essentialism demand.

IV. THINGS IN THEMSELVES

The connection between categorial description and metaphysical realism was made through the thesis that concepts are, if not sufficient, at least an integral and necessary condition for facts to exist. Our concepts mould reality, so that without concepts there can be no facts. This thesis, conceptual realism, goes beyond the claim that facts can only be *known* by people possessing the right concepts, a claim which is hardly disputable. Conceptual realism takes the possession of concepts to be a condition for the facts themselves to exist.

But if concepts mould reality are there not some pretty dire consequences for our knowledge of it? Does the thesis of conceptual realism not imply that reality, *real* reality which lies outside of concepts and is moulded by them to produce the facts, is going to remain forever hidden from us? And what is more, doesn't it imply that what *is* known, the facts produced by our concepts, is not *real* reality after all but just an illusion? Conceptual realism seems to bring with it the kind of speculative metaphysical division between appearance and reality which categorial description hoped to avoid. Kant, for example, quite explicitly adopted this sort of duality of appearance and reality; and he connected it with a theory of the conceptual construction of appearance by the mind out of the data resulting from the action on itself by mind-independent reality. Appearance and reality, phenomena and noumena, experience and things as they really are in themselves: this kind of duality seemed an inevitable consequence of giving an active role to the mind in perception. Reality seemed hidden behind a 'veil of perception' and all that was experienced was an illusory construction.

Let me make plain then that conceptual realism need not push us along that path, since it need not involve the thought that *real* reality is moulded to produce the facts. This is not because the facts are illusions built from illusions, but because the facts *are* reality. The notion of moulding reality is easily misleading, and it does mislead if it suggests that reality exists prior to its being shaped and distorted by being put into the pigeonholes provided by our concepts. The thesis of conceptual realism is indeed that pigeonholing by conceptualising is the very making of reality itself, so why should that thesis lead directly into the position taken by Kant? Suppose some objects on a table. We can describe them in various ways, say as six place settings, or Aunt Maud's best cutlery and china, or as a collection of spoons, together with a collection of knives, and so on. These facts depend upon the various concepts which are being applied, but does that mean that reality is being distorted? What is there *really* there, then, if we strip away such facts? Conceptual realism says that reality consists in those facts themselves, not that the facts hide reality from our view.

But is there no notion at work in conceptual realism of a *something* which, together with the concepts, becomes the fact? Call it what you will, this something appears to stand outside of the influence of the mind in its conceptualising activity and hence to be hidden from our ken! To relieve *this* anxiety we can admit that conceptual realism does recognise a something which becomes conceptualised: after all, facts have constituents, concepts must be applied to something to produce the facts. Yet that something does not have to be anything other than the world of tables and chairs, particulars and universals anyway. The concept of a table is applied to the *table*, and the category of particular too.[14] The concept of spatial proximity is applied to the table and the chairs. There seems no need to take the material which is conceptualised to be anything other than the world we are acquainted with.

There is a sense in which, nevertheless, a concept can be said to produce *out of something else* the thing which instantiates it. The table and the chairs are preexisting things which are brought together under the concept of a dining suite; two preexisting people are conceptualised 'as one' under the concepts of employer and employee. New facts are made out of old ones. But this is not enough to feed anxieties about a world of noumena.

Or is it? Perhaps it does not look threatening since the concepts in the examples are already fairly high-level ones, riding well up from the basic kind of conceptualising at the bottom of the ladder. There, surely, there is a level of preconceptualised reality. Well yes, insofar as there must be things and properties, events and times and place, which provide the furniture of the world and which can be variously reconceptualised to make a richer tapestry. Yet these things themselves are already concept-involving. The categories perform this function for us, not admittedly on their own without the more detailed material of concepts like chair and table; but it could be said that the categories, being the most fundamental of our concepts, have a fundamental role to play here. The picture of the ladder with a bottom rung of categories is wrong, though. Categories are fundamental concepts to be sure, but that does not mean they are at the bottom of a conceptualising ladder like that. This should be obvious from the example of the dining suite, for there a new particular is constructed from preexisting ones. The particular emerges at a higher level, not at the bottom of a conceptualising ladder. Properties, too, arise like that: natural kinds are hardly the first and simplest of the properties to be found in nature, or in the mind.

It must be admitted, nevertheless, that any account of reality has to recognise a world which predates and inevitably far exceeds the concepts we have for its description, a world which is a 'raw unexperienced welter of objects and events' in Dan O'Connor's words.[15] This *status rerum* – his term, with acknowledgement to C. K. Ogden, for what there is before conceptualisation – need present no fears of the dualist kind and no 'reality' which is more real than our own. Our world is no more than that *status rerum* suitably conceptualised, so offers no challenge to it of any sort. It is not as though the world is this-way-or-that before concepts are applied: it is, rather, this-way-or-that since concepts are applied. The notion of the *status rerum* is no more than corelative to that of the world's conceptualisation, for the latter operates upon the former.

NOTES AND REFERENCES

1 CATEGORIAL DESCRIPTION

1. Aristotle, *Categories* 1b25: the quotation is taken from the translation, with notes, by J. L. Ackrill, *Aristotle's Categories and De Interpretatione* (Oxford University Press, 1963), p. 5.
2. J. L. Ackrill, op. cit., p. 78.
3. I. Kant, *Critique of Pure Reason*, 2nd edn (J. F. Hartknoch, Riga, 1787). These categories are listed in the first chapter of the section called 'Analytic of Concepts'.
4. Ibid.
5. R. G. Collingwood, *Essay on Metaphysics* (Oxford University Press, 1940).
6. I. Kant, op. cit., 'Analytic of Principles'.
7. P. F. Strawson, *Individuals* (Methuen, London, 1959) p. 9.
8. Ibid., pp. 9–10.
9. Ibid., p. 10.
10. I. Kant, op. cit., 'Analytic of Concepts'.
11. R. Descartes, *Meditations on First Philosophy* (Paris, 1641). References are to the translation of the 2nd edition (1642) included in E. Anscombe and P. T. Geach, translators and editors, *Descartes: Philosophical Writings* (Nelson, London, 1964).
12. R. Descartes, ibid., p. 67.
13. B. Williams, *Descartes: The Project of Pure Enquiry* (Penguin, Harmondsworth, 1978) p. 112.
14. R. Descartes, op. cit., p. 61.
15. R. Descartes, op. cit., p. 114.
16. E. Anscombe and P. T. Geach, op. cit., pp. 193–4.
17. A category account of facts is presented in D. W. Hamlyn, 'The Correspondence Theory of Truth', *Philosophical Quarterly*, XII (1962), pp. 193–205.
18. G. E. Moore, *Principia Ethica* (Cambridge University Press, 1903).

2 SUBSTANCE

1. Aristotle, *Categories* 2a11: J. L. Ackrill, op. cit., p. 5.
2. This interpretation is taken in J. L. Mackie, *Problems from Locke* (Oxford University Press, 1976), pp. 73–6.

3. J. Locke, *An Essay Concerning Human Understanding*, 2 vols (London, 1690). This quotation is from the 5th edition of 1706, reprinted in the Everyman's Library, edited by J. W. Yolton (Dent, London, 1961), Vol. I, p. 245.

4. J. Locke, op. cit., p. 245.

5. L. Wittgenstein, *Tractatus Logico-Philosophicus*, first edition in *Annalen der Naturphilosophie* 1921: quotations are from the D. F. Pears and B. F. McGuiness translation (Routledge & Kegan Paul, London, 1961).

6. B. Russell, *The Philosophy of Logical Atomism*, first published 1918: a convenient edition is D. F. Pears (ed.), *Russell's Logical Atomism* (Fontana, London, 1972).

7. B. Russell, *Introduction to Mathematical Philosophy* (Allen & Unwin, London, 1920), p. 173.

8. G. W. Leibniz, *Monadology* (Paris, 1714). This quotation is from G. H. R. Parkinson (ed.), *Leibniz: Philosophical Writings* (Dent, London, 1973), p.179.

9. G. W. Leibniz, *Discourse on Metaphysics* (1686). This quotation is from G. H. R. Parkinson (ed.), op. cit., pp. 18–19.

10. G. W. Leibniz, *Discourse*, (ed.) G. H. R. Parkinson, op. cit., p. 18.

11. S. A. Kripke, *Naming and Necessity* (1970). These lectures, originally delivered at Princeton University, are reprinted in S. A. Kripke, *Naming and Necessity* (Blackwell, Oxford, 1980) from which quotations are taken. Other major proponents of modern essentialism are Hilary Putnam, David Lewis and Alvin Plantinga: see works by them included in the Bibliography below.

12. Ibid., p. 113.

13. Such an appreciation does, of course, involve many false assumptions about the past: the point is that these false beliefs are shared and form part of the background of our use of names.

14. S. A. Kripke, op. cit., p. 15.

15. Ibid., p. 19.

16. J. S. Mill, *A System of Logic* (8th edition Longman, London, 1872) p. 15.

17. P. F. Strawson, op. cit., pp. 187–8.

18. Ibid., p. 167.

3 ESSENCE AND ACCIDENT

1. G. Berkeley, *Treatise Concerning the Principles of Human Knowledge* (1710), especially the introduction; this work is included in the Everyman's Library collection, *Berkeley: A New Theory of Vision and Other Writings* (Dent, London, 1957): D. Hume, *Treatise of Human Nature* (1739), Book I, Part I, Section VII; an easily available edition is L. Selby-Bigge (ed.), *David Hume: Treatise of Human Nature* (Oxford University Press, 1967).

2. See e.g. Plato, *Republic* Book Five: translated with an introduction by Desmond Lee (Penguin, Harmondsworth, 1955).

3. See e.g. Plato, *Parmenides* in E. Hamilton and H. Cairns (eds), *Plato: The Collected Dialogues* (Pantheon Books, New York, 1961).

4. Aristotle, *Metaphysics* Book VII: in R. McKeon (ed.), *The Basic Works of Aristotle* (Random House, New York, 1941).

5. B. Russell, *Problems of Philosophy* (Oxford University Press, 1959) p. 55.

6. Aristotle, *Posterior Analytics* Book II, Chapter 19: in R. McKeon, op. cit.

7. G. W. Leibniz, *Monadology*, (ed.) G. H. R. Parkinson, op. cit., p. 185.

8. See the papers collected in S. P. Swartz (ed.), *Naming, Necessity and Natural Kinds* (Cornell University Press, 1977).

9. J. L. Mackie, *Problems from Locke*, (Oxford University Press, 1976) p. 87.

10. J. Locke, *Essay*, Vol. I, pp. 131–2.

11. J. Locke, *Essay*, Vol. II, p. 42ff.

12. Ibid., Chapter III.

13. J. Locke, *Essay*, Vol. II, p. 23.

14. J. Locke, *Essay*, Vol. I, p. 320.

15. S. A. Kripke, op. cit., Lecture III *passim*.

16. J. L. Mackie, op. cit., p. 93ff.

17. S. A. Kripke, op. cit., p. 12.

18. Dan O'Connor has pointed out to me that we should, on the rigid designator approach, allow for possible worlds in which things do not even *have* a real essence different from their nominal essence: that is to say, the interiors of all substances are totally unstructured and consist of unanalysable mush. Such worlds would still operate as causal systems but no rationale of such would exist. In such possible worlds (of which there could be an uncountable multitude) macrostructure and behaviour would not be explicable in terms of microstructure and micromechanisms. To such worlds what relevance could our scientific vocabulary possibly have? He reminds me, too, that in our world there are many complications which our scientific classifications need to note – isomers, allotropes and isotopes included.

19. R. Harré and E. H. Madden, *Causal Powers: A Theory of Natural Necessity* (Blackwell, Oxford, 1975), *passim*.

4 CAUSATION

1. J. L. Ackrill, *Aristotle the Philosopher* (Oxford University Press, 1981), p. 36.

2. Aristotle, *Physics* Book II, Ch. 3: this translation is from J. Barnes, *Aristotle* (Oxford University Press, 1982), p. 52.

3. J. Locke, *Essay*, Book II, Ch. XXI. The next three quotations are from that chapter and the following one.

4. D. Hume, *An Inquiry Concerning Human Understanding*, 1748: edited with an introduction by C. W. Hendel (Bobbs-Merrill, New York, 1955), pp. 87–8.

5. Ibid., p. 75. The following quotation is from the same page.

6. D. Hume, *Treatise*, p. 682.

7. D. Hume, *Inquiry*, p. 77. The next two quotations are from p. 85 and p. 87 respectively.

8. D. Hume, *Treatise*, p. 170.

9. Ibid., p. 156.

10. Ibid., p. 165.

11. D. Hume, *Inquiry*, p. 87.

12. J. S. Mill, *System of Logic*, p. 214. All quotations are from that and the following three pages.

13. R. G. Collingwood, 'On the So-Called Idea of Causation', *Proceedings of the Aristotelian Society*, Vol. XXXVIII (1938).

14. H. L. A. Hart and A. M. Honoré, *Causation in the Law* (Oxford University Press, 1959), p. 42.

15. J. S. Mill, op. cit., p. 222.

16. J. L. Mackie, 'Causes and Conditions', *American Philosophical Quarterly*, Vol. 2 (1965): reprinted in E. Sosa (ed.), *Causation and Conditionals* (Oxford University Press, 1975).

17. J. L. Mackie, *The Cement of the Universe* (Oxford University Press, 1974).

18. R. Harré and E. H. Madden, *Causal Powers* (Blackwell, Oxford, 1975).

19. Ibid., p. 7.

20. Ibid., p. 44.

21. J. L. Mackie, *The Cement of the Universe*.

22. D. Lewis, *Counterfactuals* (Blackwell, Oxford, 1973).

23. Ibid., p. 16.

24. See R. C. Stalnaker, 'A Theory of Conditionals' in N. Rescher (ed.), *Studies in Logical Theory* (Blackwell, Oxford, 1968); reprinted in E. Sosa, op. cit.

25. Ibid., p. 57.

26. Ibid., p. 24.

27. Ibid., p. 26.

28. Ibid., p. 85.

29. Ibid., p. 87.

30. Ibid., p. 84.

5 SPACE AND TIME

1. Once more I exclude from consideration those peculiar entities called numbers.

2. On the history of the philosophy of space and time in Greek thought, see the articles in P. Edwards (ed.), *Encyclopedia of Philosophy* (Collier Macmillan, London) by J. J. C. Smart, 'Space' and 'Time'; and works on Greek philosophy generally, such as J. Burnet, *Early Greek Philosophy*, 3rd edition (Black, London, 1920).

3. Aristotle, *Physics*, Book IV: this translation is by R. P. Hardie and R. C. Gaye, in *The Works of Aristotle*, ed. W. D. Ross (Oxford University Press, 1930).

4. Ibid.

5. O. R. Frisch, 'Parity Not Conserved, a New Twist to Physics?', *University Quarterly*, Vol. 11 (1957), pp. 235–44.

6. See, e.g., A. Grunbaum, 'Carnap's Views on the Foundations of Geometry' in P. A. Schilpp (ed.), *The Philosophy of Rudolf Carnap* (Open Court, LaSalle, 1964).

7. B. Russell, *Our Knowledge and the External World* (Allen & Unwin, London, 1922). The lecture on 'The Problem of Infinity Considered Historically' is reprinted in J. J. C. Smart (ed.), *Problems of Space and Time* (Macmillan, New York, 1964) from which the quotation is taken, p. 156. An

excellent and detailed account of Zeno's paradoxes is G. Vlastos, 'Zeno of Elea' in the *Encyclopedia of Philosophy*.

8. J. M. E. McTaggart, 'The Unreality of Time', *Mind*, Vol. 17 (1908); reprinted in his *Philosophical Studies* (Arnold, London, 1934). The argument is repeated in his *The Nature of Existence*, Vol. ii (Cambridge University Press, 1927), Book v, Ch. 33.

9. J. M. E. McTaggart, *The Nature of Existence*, Book v, Ch. 33: reprinted in R. M. Gale (ed.), *The Philosophy of Time* (Macmillan, London, 1968), this quotation being from that reprint, p. 88.

10. Ibid., p. 89.

11. Ibid., pp. 90–1.

12. B. Russell, *Principles of Mathematics* (Cambridge University Press, 1903): quoted in J. M. E. McTaggart, op. cit., p. 92.

13. Ibid., p. 92.

14. Ibid., pp. 94–5.

15. Ibid., p. 95.

16. Ibid., pp. 95–6.

17. Ibid., p. 96.

18. See, e.g., various papers in R. M. Gale (ed.), *The Philosophy of Time* and others mentioned in that book's bibliography.

19. H. G. Alexander (ed.), *The Leibniz-Clarke Correspondence* (Manchester University Press, 1956). This exchange took place in 1715 and 1716, and was first published by Clarke in 1717.

20. This quotation is taken from the reprint of Leibniz's Third Paper in J. J. C. Smart (ed.), *Problems of Space and Time* (Macmillan, New York, 1964), pp. 89–90.

21. Ibid., p. 90.

22. Ibid., p. 89.

23. C. D. Broad, *Leibniz: An Introduction* (Cambridge University Press, 1975), p. 59.

24. H. G. Alexander, op. cit., p. xxxvi of Alexander's introduction. This whole introduction is worth reading as a guide to the debate between Leibniz and the Newtonians, and the fate of that debate through to the present century. My own account owes something, though not everything, to Alexander's.

25. Newton's arguments can be found in the Scholium to the Definitions in his *Mathematical Principles of Natural Philosophy*, first published in 1687. Relevant sections are reprinted in J. J. C. Smart (ed.), op. cit. , pp. 81–8. For brevity and simplicity of exposition I have omitted Newton's arguments for absolute time.

26. E. Mach, *The Science of Mechanics* (Leibzig, 1883). Relevant sections are reprinted in J. J. C. Smart (ed.), op. cit., pp. 126–31. This specific question is put on pp. 129–30.

27. I. Kant, *Prolegomena to Any Future Metaphysics*, first published in 1783: translated and edited by P. G. Lucas (Manchester University Press, 1953), pp. 41–3.

28. I. Kant, *Critique of Pure Reason*, section entitled 'Transcendental Aesthetic'. What follows is an oversimplified sketch of Kant's argument,

which fits more closely his account of space and geometry than his account of time and arithmetic.

29. I. Kant, *Critique*, pp. 86–7.

30. Ibid., p. 72.

31. Developments in science since Kant's time have involved a major shift in our attitude to the mathematical sciences, particularly though not exclusively in our appreciation of the extent to which a choice of geometry is a matter for physical science. See various papers by Eddington, Nagel, Reichenbach et al. reprinted in J. J. C. Smart (ed.), *Problems of Space and Time*.

32. I. Kant, *Critique*, pp. 69–70.

33. A. Quinton, 'Spaces and Times', *Philosophy*, Vol. 37 (1962).

34. Ibid., p. 136.

35. Ibid., p. 139.

36. Ibid., p. 144.

37. Ibid., p. 145.

38. Ibid., p. 146.

39. R. G. Swinburne, 'Times', *Analysis*, 25.6 (1965), p. 186. Swinburne's second thoughts on his argument are contained in his *Space and Time* (Macmillan, London, 1968).

40. Ibid., p. 190.

6 METAPHYSICAL TRUTH

1. Strawson's arguments are contained in *Individuals*, especially Chapters 1–4. Kant's arguments are in *Critique of Pure Reason* especially the section called 'Analytic of Principles'.

2. D. W. Hamlyn, *Theory of Knowledge* (Macmillan, London, 1970), pp. 68–75, 136–42. See also his Inaugural Lecture at Birkbeck College, London University, 'Seeing Things As They Are' (1965).

3. L. Wittgenstein, *Philosophical Investigations*, 1953 (2nd edn: Blackwell, Oxford, 1963), paragraph 580.

4. Ibid., paragraphs 240–315.

5. See, for example, R. Albritton, 'On Wittgenstein's Use of the Term "Criterion" ', *Journal of Philosophy*, Vol. LXI (1959) pp. 845–57; reprinted with a postscript in G. Pitcher (ed.), *Wittgenstein: The Philosophical Investigations* (Macmillan, London, 1968).

6. D. W. Hamlyn, op. cit., p. 71.

7. Ibid., pp. 201–2.

8. See articles on this question in G. Pitcher (ed.), *Wittgenstein: The Philosophical Investigations* and in O. R. Jones (ed.), *The Private Language Argument* (Macmillan, London, 1971).

9. On this idea, which among other things creates difficulties for the Logical Positivists' equation of meaningfulness and verifiability, compare G. Langford, 'Impossible Knowledge', *Religious Studies*, Vol. 10 (1973), pp. 213–18.

10. Examples of such changes were given in Chapter 1, section I.4. Further development of the position of conceptual realism should involve the differences between concepts (e.g. unicorn) which are acknowledged to have

no instances and those which do, and comparably the distinction between retired concepts (e.g. witch) which had no warrant for their application and those (e.g. phlogiston) which had.

11. For example A. J. Ayer, *Language, Truth and Logic* (Gollancz, London, 1936: Penguin, Harmondsworth, 1971).

12. I. Kant, *Critique of Pure Reason*, section called 'Transcendental Dialectic'.

13. D. Hume, *Inquiry*, p. 173.

14. This is consistent with a concept, such as acid, being later applied to more things than those which originally fell under it.

15. D. J. O'Connor, *Correspondence Theory of Truth* (Hutchinson, London, 1975) p. 130.

Bibliography

Ackrill, J. L. (ed.), *Aristotle's Categories and De Interpretatione* (Oxford University Press, 1963)

Ackrill, J. L., *Aristotle the Philosopher* (Oxford University Press, 1981)

Alexander, H. G. (ed.), *The Leibniz–Clarke Correspondence* (Manchester University Press, 1956)

Alexander, S., *Space Time and Deity*, 2 vols (Macmillan, London, 1920)

Anscombe, E. and Geach, P. T. (trs and eds), *Descartes: Philosophical Writings* (Nelson, London, 1964)

Anscombe, G. E. M., *Metaphysics and the Philosophy of Mind* (Blackwell, Oxford, 1981)

Armstrong, D. M., *Universals and Scientific Realism*, 2 vols (Cambridge University Press, 1978)

Atkinson, R. F. A., *Knowledge and Explanation in History* (Macmillan, London, 1978)

Ayer, A. J., *Language, Truth and Logic* (Gollancz, London, 1936; Penguin, Harmondsworth, 1971)

Barnes, J., *Aristotle* (Oxford University Press, 1982)

Bergson, H., *Time and Free-will* (Allen & Unwin, London, 1911)

Bradley, F. H., *Appearance and Reality* (Allen & Unwin, London, 1920)

Bradley, R. and Swartz, N., *Possible Worlds* (Blackwell, Oxford, 1979)

Broad, C. D., *An Examination of McTaggart's Philosophy*, 3 vols (Cambridge University Press, 1933–8)

Brody, B. A., *Identity and Essence* (Princeton University Press, 1980)

Butchvarov, P., *Resemblance and Identity* (Indiana University Press, 1966)

Campbell, K., *Metaphysics: An Introduction* (Dickenson, Encino, California, 1976)

Carnap, R., *Meaning and Necessity* (Chicago University Press, 1947)

Carr, B., *Bertrand Russell* (Allen & Unwin, London, 1975)

Carr, B. and O'Connor, D. J., *Introduction to the Theory of Knowledge* (Harvester, Brighton, 1982; Minnesota University Press, 1982)

Chisholm, R. M., *Person and Object* (Allen & Unwin, London, 1976)

Chisholm, R. M. and Guterman, N., (trs and eds), *F. Brentano: The Theory of Categories 1907–17* (Martinus Nijhoff, The Hague, 1981)

Collingwood, R. G., *An Essay on Metaphysics* (Oxford University Press, 1940)

Davidson, D., *Essays on Actions and Events* (Oxford University Press, 1980)

Davidson, D. and Harman, G. (eds), *Semantics of Natural Languages* (Reidel, Dordrecht, 1972)

Davies, M., *Meaning, Quantification, Necessity* (Routledge & Kegan Paul, London, 1981)

Denbigh, K. G., *Three Concepts of Time* (Springer-Verlag, New York, 1981)

Dummett, M., *Truth and Other Enigmas* (Duckworth, London, 1978)

Edwards, P. (ed.), *Encyclopedia of Philosophy*, 8 vols (Collier Macmillan, London, 1967; Macmillan & Free Press, New York, 1967)

Elwes, R. H. M. (tr. and ed.), *Benedict de Spinoza: On the Improvement of the Understanding* (and other works) (Dover, New York, 1955)

Emmet, D. M., *The Nature of Metaphysical Thinking* (Macmillan, London, 1945)

Ewing, A. C., *Idealism: A Critical Study* (Methuen, London, 1934)

Fisk, M., *Nature and Necessity* (Indiana University Press, 1973)

Freeman, E. and Sellars W. (eds), *Basic Issues in the Philosophy of Time* (Open Court, LaSalle, 1971)

Gale, R. M., *The Language of Time* (Routledge & Kegan Paul, London, 1968)

Gale, R. M. (ed.), *The Philosophy of Time* (Macmillan, London, 1968)

Geach, P. T., *Reference and Generality* (Cornell University Press, Ithaca, N.Y., 1962)

Grossmann, R., *Ontological Reduction* (Indiana University Press, 1973)

Grunbaum, A., *Philosophical Problems of Space and Time* (Knopf, New York, 1963)

Hamilton E. and Cairns H. (eds), *Plato: The Collected Dialogues* (Pantheon, New York, 1961)

Hamlyn, D. W., *Metaphysics* (Cambridge University Press, 1984)

Hamlyn, D. W., *Theory of Knowledge* (Macmillan, London, 1971)

Hampshire, S., *Thought and Action* (Chatto & Windus, London, 1959)

Harré, R. and Madden, E. H., *Causal Powers: A Theory of Natural Necessity* (Blackwell, Oxford, 1975)

Harrison, R., *On What There Must Be* (Oxford University Press, 1974)

Hart, H. L. A. and Honoré, A. M., *Causation in the Law* (Oxford University Press, 1959)

Hendel, C. W. (ed.), *Hume: An Inquiry Concerning Human Understanding* (Bobbs-Merrill, New York, 1955)

Hinckfuss, I., *The Existence of Space and Time* (Oxford University Press, 1975)

Jones, O. R. (ed.), *The Private Language Argument* (Macmillan, London, 1971)

Kemp Smith, N. (ed.), *Kant: Critique of Pure Reason*, 2nd edn, 1787 (Macmillan, London, 1964)

Korner, S., *Conceptual Thinking*, 2nd edn (Dover, New York, 1959)

Korner, S., *Categorial Frameworks* (Blackwell, Oxford, 1970)

Korner, S., *Metaphysics: its Structure and Function* (Cambridge University Press, 1984)

Kripke, S. A., *Naming and Necessity*, 1970 (Oxford University Press, 1980)

Langford, G., *Education, Persons and Society* (Macmillan, London, 1985)

Langford, G., *Human Action* (Macmillan, London, 1972)

Lewis, D., *Counterfactuals* (Blackwell, Oxford, 1973)

Loux, M. J. (ed.), *Universals and Particulars: Readings in Ontology* (Doubleday, New York, 1970)

Loux, M. J. *Substance and Attribute* (Reidel, Dordrecht, 1978)

Lucas, J. R., *A Treatise on Time and Space* (Methuen, London, 1973)

Lucas, P. G. (tr. and ed.), *Immanuel Kant: Prolegomena* (Manchester University Press, 1953)

Mackie J. L., *Problems from Locke* (Oxford University Press, 1976)

Mackie, J. L., *The Cement of the Universe* (Oxford University Press, 1974)

Mackie, J. L., *Truth, Probability and Paradox* (Oxford University Press, 1973)

McKeon, R. (ed.), *The Basic Works of Aristotle* (Random House, New York, 1941)

McTaggart, J. M. E., *The Nature of Existence*, 2 vols (Cambridge University Press, 1927)

Mahalingam, I., *Communication Without Language: A Framework* (Unpublished Ph.D. thesis, Exeter University, 1983)

Margolis, J. (ed.), *Fact and Existence* (Blackwell, Oxford, 1969)

Martin, G., *General Metaphysics* (Allen & Unwin, London, 1968)

Mellor, D. H., *Real Time* (Cambridge University Press, 1981)

Mill, J. S., *A System of Logic*, 1843, 8th edn (Longman, London, 1872)

Moore, G. E., *Principia Ethica* (Cambridge University Press, 1903)

Munitz, M. K., *Existence and Logic* (New York University Press, 1974)

Munitz, M. K. (ed.), *Identity and Individuation* (New York University Press, 1971)

Munitz, M. K., *Space, Time and Creation* (Free Press, Glencoe, 1957)

Nerlich, G., *The Shape of Space* (Cambridge University Press, 1976)

Newton-Smith, W. H., *The Structure of Time* (Routledge & Kegan Paul, London, 1980)

Noonan, H. W., *Objects and Identity* (Martinus Nijhoff, The Hague, 1980)

Norreklit, L., *Concepts* (Odense University Press, 1973)

O'Connor, D. J. (ed.), *A Critical History of Western Philosophy* (Free Press, Glencoe, 1964; Macmillan, London, 1985)

O'Connor, D. J., *The Correspondence Theory of Truth* (Hutchinson, London, 1975)

O'Connor, D. J. and Carr, B., *Introduction to the Theory of Knowledge* (Harvester, Brighton, 1982; Minnesota University Press, 1982)

Parkinson, G. H. R. (ed.), *Leibniz: Philosophical Writings* (Dent, London, 1973)

Pearce, G. and Maynard, P. (eds), *Conceptual Change* (Reidel, Dordrecht, 1973)

Pears, D. F. (ed.), *The Nature of Metaphysics* (Macmillan, London, 1960)

Pears, D. F. (ed.), *Russell's Logical Atomism* (Fontana, London, 1972)

Pitcher, G. (ed.), *Truth* (Prentice-Hall, Englewood Cliffs, N.J., 1964)

Pitcher G. (ed.), *Wittgenstein: the Philosophical Investigations* (Macmillan, London, 1968)

Plantinga, A., *The Nature of Necessity* (Oxford University Press, 1974)

Putnam, H., *Mind, Language and Reality: Philosophical Papers Vol. 2* (Cambridge University Press, 1975)

Putnam, H., *Reason, Truth and History* (Cambridge University Press, 1981)

Quine, W. V. O., *Word and Object* (M.I.T. Press, Cambridge, Mass., 1960)

Quine, W. V. O., *Ontological Relativity and Other Essays* (Columbia University Press, New York, 1969)

Quinton, A. M., *The Nature of Things* (Routledge & Kegan Paul, London, 1973)

Reichenbach, H., *The Philosophy of Space and Time* (Dover, New York, 1957)

Reichenbach, H., *The Direction of Time* (University of California Press, Berkeley, 1971)

Rescher, N., *Conceptual Idealism* (Blackwell, Oxford, 1973)

Russell, B., *Problems of Philosophy*, 1912 (Oxford University Press, 1959)

Salmon, W. C., *Space, Time and Motion* (Dickenson, Encino, California, 1975)

Selby-Bigge, L. (ed.), *David Hume: Treatise of Human Nature*, 1739–40 (Oxford University Press, 1888)

Schlesinger, G. N., *Metaphysics* (Blackwell, Oxford, 1983)

Sellars, W., *Science and Metaphysics* (Routledge & Kegan Paul, London, 1968)

Sklar, R., *Space, Time and Spacetime* (University of California Press, 1974)

Slote, M. A., *Metaphysics and Essence* (Blackwell, Oxford, 1974)

Smart, J. J. C. (ed.), *Problems of Space and Time* (Collier-Macmillan, New York, 1964)

Sosa, E. (ed.), *Causation and Conditionals* (Oxford University Press, 1975)

Sprague, E., *Metaphysical Thinking* (Oxford University Press, New York, 1978)

Staniland, H., *Universals* (Macmillan, London, 1973)

Strawson, P. F., *Individuals* (Methuen, London, 1959)

Strawson, P. F., *Introduction to Logical Theory* (Methuen, London, 1952)

Strawson, P. F., *Logico-Linguistic Papers* (Methuen, London, 1971)

Strawson, P. F., *Subject and Predicate in Logic and Grammar* (Methuen, London, 1974)

Strawson, P. F., *The Bounds of Sense* (Methuen, London, 1968)

Suppes, P. (ed.), *Space, Time and Geometry* (Reidel, Dordrecht, 1973)

Swartz, S. P. (ed.), *Naming, Necessity and Natural Kinds* (Cornell University Press, 1977)

Swinburne, R., *Space and Time* (Macmillan, London, 1968)

Taylor, R., *Metaphysics* (Prentice-Hall, Englewood Cliffs, N.Y., 1963)

Van Fraassen, B. C., *An Introduction to the Philosophy of Space and Time* (Random House, New York, 1970)

Van Inwagen, P. (ed.), *Time and Cause* (Reidel, Dordrecht, 1980)

Walsh, W. H., *Metaphysics* (Hutchinson, London, 1963)

Walsh, W. H., *Kant's Criticism of Metaphysics* (Edinburgh University Press, 1975)

Warnock, G. J. (ed.), *George Berkeley: The Principles of Human Knowledge*, (1710) with other writings (Fontana, London 1962)

White, A. R., *Truth* (Macmillan, London, 1971)

Whitrow, G. J., *The Natural Philosophy of Space and Time* (Oxford University Press, 1980)

Williams, B., *Descartes: The Project of Pure Enquiry* (Penguin, Harmondsworth, 1978)

Wiggins, D., *Identity and Spatiotemporal Continuity* (Blackwell, Oxford, 1967)

Wiggins, D., *Sameness and Substance* (Blackwell, Oxford, 1980)

Wittgenstein, L., *Philosophical Investigations* 1953, 2nd edn (Blackwell, Oxford, 1963)

Wittgenstein, L., *Tractatus Logico-Philosophicus*, 1921 (Routledge & Kegan Paul, London, 1961)

Wolterstorff, N., *On Universals* (Chicago University Press, 1970)

Yolton, J. W. (ed.), *John Locke: An Essay Concerning Human Understanding*, 2 vols, 5th edn (Dent, London, 1961)

Yolton, J. W., *Metaphysical Analysis* (Allen & Unwin, London, 1968)

INDEX